Andreas Simon

Chicago, the Garden City

Its Magnificent Parks, Boulevards and Cemeteries...

Andreas Simon

Chicago, the Garden City
Its Magnificent Parks, Boulevards and Cemeteries...

ISBN/EAN: 9783337013875

Printed in Europe, USA, Canada, Australia, Japan

Cover: Foto ©Andreas Hilbeck / pixelio.de

More available books at **www.hansebooks.com**

CHICAGO

THE GARDEN CITY.

Its Magnificent Parks, Boulevards and Cemeteries.

~~~

-- TOGETHER WITH OTHER --

DESCRIPTIVE VIEWS AND SKETCHES.

Profusely Illustrated.

~~~

COMPILED AND EDITED

BY ANDREAS SIMON.

CHICAGO:
THE FRANZ GINDELE PRINTING CO.,
140-146 Monroe Street.
1893.

CONTENTS.

ILLUSTRATIONS.

PREFACE.

THE admirable and extensive Park System of the "Fair" City testifies loudly to the fact that the legislative authorities of the State of Illinois had early recognized the high value of public gardens and the sanitary benefits which large cities derive therefrom.

Ample provision is made that our parks, the "lungs" of this large city, are from year to year enriched by new charms and additional landscape scenery, thanks to the munificence of the people who every year pay many thousands of dollars into the treasury of the park commissioners. The fact is conceded by all that the parks are a necessity for the health of the people and a means for their moral and æsthetic education.

Every human being, who has an open heart for the beauties and joys of nature is gladdened when he gives himself up to the agreeable influences of these shady groves, for they help him to forget and bear more easily the troubles and cares of every day life. Soothed and with new vigor of body and soul he returns to his accustomed occupation.

What then could be offered to the masses in large cities, earning their daily bread in the sweat of their brow, that would be more pleasant and beneficial than the opportunity to spend their short hours of recreation in the glorious temple of nature with its innocent and precious joys?

Of special value are our parks to the people of Chicago on Sundays and Holidays. Then they pour into these lovely groves on foot and in carriages to enjoy there the cool shade of the trees, the sight of the many colored flower beds and the purer air. This is indeed a recreation for the toiling laborer and where else could it be found within his reach, but in these gardens which are so richly endowed by nature and art? And what a refreshing spring of health and pleasure these parks are for the children!

They indeed prove a great blessing to all the people, and especially to those who between Sundays and Holidays are huddled together in dingy quarters and are exercising and tasking all their strength to keep want from their threshold. The pure fresh air, laden with the fragrance of flowers, the elevating sight of the green meadows, the groves with their feathered songsters, the flowers, and the ponds with the swiftly flying boats plowing their mirror-like surface, give new courage and hope to the faint hearts; and the children of the poor classes, growing up amongst want and privations in unhealthy hovels, generally preys to disease during the hot days of summer, gather new strength here, and the refreshing air, fanning their feverish cheeks, together with the sights of all the beauties of nature bring sunshine and joy to these little sick and feeble ones, and in many cases no doubt health again, too.

Extraordinary exertions were made last year (1892) not only to give the several parks increased scenic charms but also to complete before the opening of the Exposition the chain of boulevards winding around the city as an incomparable beautiful cycle of green gardens.

Mr. John Thorpe, who knows perhaps more about flowers than any other man in this country and who for this reason was selected as chief of floriculture by the Director-general of the World's Columbian Exposition, has the following to say in regard to our parks and their floral decorations:

"Owing in great part to its geographical position there is probably no city in the Union whose Public Parks are as varied and interesting as those of Chicago. Each Park has its well known individual features and distinct characteristics, the result of their having been planned and laid out in each case under entirely different management.

Humboldt Park is particularly rich in natural landscape and the leading feature of Lincoln Park is found in its superb water effects. Douglas and Garfield Park each have attractive features purely their own, while Washington Park probably derives its great popularity from the magnificent way in which temporary material, flowering and bedding plants, are shown during the spring, summer and autumn, of each year.

I am aware that the general work done in the Chicago Parks, and especially that done by Mr. Fred Kanst, the Superintendent of Washington Park, has been criticized by writers in some of the leading publications of the country, but I feel that it is unjust to make such severe criticisms on work which is artistic in its way and no more counterfeit than is a portrait on canvas. I feel that many people would prevent children from seeing a chromo or a lithograph because their parents were not sufficiently rich to buy a Corot or a Turner picture. It is a strange fact that of the hundreds of thousands of people, who visit the Chicago Parks, the large majority of them visit and linger most around the very features, which these so called critics condemn and it is in this vicinity, that the grass is trodden down almost beyond recognition under the feet of the great masses of people, who gather there to enjoy these very effects; thus showing the great interest that is taken therein by the very people to whose pleasure and enjoyment it is the main purpose of the Public Parks to cater.

It must be understood that there is a great deal of flower planting done that is as free from geometry as are natures groupings, so there is no fear of there being one class of work neglected to the advantage or disparagement of another."

And the skillful florists of the several parks are determined to make a much finer show this year of flower decorations, than ever before.

It is the purpose of this book not only to be a guide for the many World's Fair visitors to and through the parks and boulevards and its park-like cemeteries, but also to furnish needed information regarding the beauties and peculiarities, the size and arrangements of these public gardens and the astonishing progress made in landscape gardening. With the conviction that such a description of our beautiful and much praised park and cemetery-system, as it is now seen in its perfection, is calculated to awaken interest in and strengthen the love for this beautiful city, which will in itself during 1893 be the most wonderful and curious object on exhibition, this book is submitted to an indulgent public and to all friends of nature by

THE AUTHOR.

Our Beautiful Parks.

Lincoln Park.—Equestrian Statue of General Grant.

LINCOLN PARK.

All of our beautiful parks give evidence, that their high sanitary value was already fully recognized at a time, when Chicago was yet numbered among the smaller cities of our country, but none enjoy greater popularity among the people from abroad, as well as among those from our own city, as Lincoln Park, over on the North Side, where the foaming billows of mighty Lake Michigan break over the rocky beach of this magnificent stretch of park-land and moisten it with their spray.

The first move made in the direction of establishing Lincoln Park is found in the records of the Council proceedings of 1860, where a memorial is found signed by George Manierre, William Jones, Benjamin W Raymond, Walter L. Newberry, Grant Goodrich and Mark Skinner (those pioneers and earliest workers for Chicago's present greatness, but who all now lie in their silent graves), stating that the cemetery, located then upon the 60 acres now forming the extreme southern part of the present park, was in a shamefully dilapidated condition and petitioning the Mayor and the city authorities to carry out in good faith their pledges to the purchasers of lots, to use the fund arising from the sale of lots in improving and keeping in repair said cemetery, and also stating that " it is not desired that there should be any extension of the limits " of the then existing cemetery grounds, and asking for the appointment of a special committee to take immediate action in the matter. In accordance with the request contained in said memorial James Long and Benjamin Carpenter were appointed such special committee to examine into and report on the matter. Jan. 10, 1860, said committee reported that negotiations were then pending with the officers of the Rosehill Cemetery company for a section of its ground wherein to bury the dead falling under the city's charge, and also to insure a place of burial for the poor. It adds: ' It seems to have become a settled thing in the public mind that no further extension of the cemetery grounds within the city limits be permitted." And it acknowledges the justice of such sentiment as follows: "That it is the sacred duty of the city to live up to its pledges and to protect, improve, and save from delapidation the spot where the remains of our early settlers lie, in order that the citizens may have the fullest confidence in its permanency. And it is further ordered that the cemetery should not be permitted to extend beyond its then limits, and that the north sixty acres should remain unoccupied.

It is stated in this letter that the ground purchased by the city comprises 120 acres; that the south sixty acres only have been subdivided into lots and sold for cemetery purposes, and after other suggestions is the following: "We propose the abandonment of this tract (the north sixty acres) to the city to be used for a public ground, and such other public purposes (if any) as the Common Council may devote it to. We do not advise its sale; such a step we think would be unwise."

On June 13, 1864, an ordinance was introduced in the city council by John M. Armstrong, of the then 13th ward, consisting of three sections as follows:

1. That hereafter no bodies shall be buried in the Chicago cemetery, except in the lots which have been sold by the city

2. All the north part of the Chicago cemetery which has not been surveyed and divided into cemetery lots (here follows the description) is hereby set apart for and declared to be a public park, and shall be known by the name of———————.

Sec. 3 provides, in substance, for the subdivision and sale of certain other property in the vicinity of the cemetery grounds, owned by the city, "the proceeds of which shall be applied to the improvement of a public park aforesaid," etc.

The matter by the records appears to have stood in this shape, it not appearing that any opposition was made; at least there is none to be found in the printed records of the Common Council until Oct. 21, 1864, when it appears that Ald. Armstrong called the matter up, and after some controversy as to the third section the first and second sections were carried unanimously and the third section rejected, and Ald. Holden moved that the blank in the second section be filled in—" Douglas Park." This was rejected by a vote of 14 to 9. Ald. Woodman moved that the park be named " Lake Park," and the said two sections were then so unanimously passed.

Subsequently July 5, 1865, the late Ald. Iver Lawson moved, that as the park on the lake front and Michigan Avenue was named " Lake Park" the said sixty acres of the cemetery grounds be known as " Lincoln Park," which was unanimously carried.

But the Armstrong ordinance, prohibiting burials in the potters' field, was almost entirely disregarded, and since its passage some 533 bodies of paupers had been buried there (sixty-three of them at the city's expense), so on Sept. 4, of that year a resolution was introduced in the Council, which was immediately passed, ordering the proper authorities to attend to the rigid enforcement of said ordinance in that regard.

As a legal proposition, the rights of the lot holders under their purchases were inalienable and could not under ordinary circumstances be interfered with. April 2, 1866, a resolution to the Common Council was immediately adopted, appointing a special committee for the purpose of consulting with the City Physician and other leading physicians as to the effect upon the general health of the city from the practice of burials in the old cemetery and the Catholic Cemetery adjoining on the south, they being so near our water supply, etc. Said committee shortly afterward reported in substance that as a sanitary measure all such burials should be prohibited as injurious to the public health, etc. Upon said report Alderman Proudfoot drew up and presented an ordinance as a sanitary measure,'prohibiting all burials, extending such prohibition to the entire limits of the City of Chicago, which was passed by a vote of 27 to 2, May 28, 1866. This put a stop to all future burials within the limits of the City of Chicago, and as a matter of course created a great deal of dissatisfaction among the majority of the purchasers of lots in the said cemetery.

Finally the authorities got the said lot owners' consent to the removal of all the bodies interred in their lots in exchange for equally valuable lots in some one or other of the new cemeteries, and the final result was that said cemetery was almost entirely vacated and handed over to the city for park purposes.

Mr. W. C. Goudy, President of the Lincoln Park Board for the last five years, who has been connected with Lincoln Park either as attorney or commissioner from the time of the passage of the original park ordinance, took an active part in originating the park system in 1863. It so happened that on a visit to the grounds, which lay between Center Street and Webster Ave., the idea occurred to him also, that the ground was suitable for a park and he accordingly examined the title of property and ascertained that it was not dedicated for a cemetery, but belonged to the city by an absolute purchase, with a right to use it for any public purpose. He then procured the active service of Voluntine C. Turner, who was then in the management of the north side street railroad, and, after having revised the ordinance, with his influence exerted upon other aldermen in aid of the efforts made by Alderman Armstrong, the ordinance was passed.

But notwithstanding the prominent part the aforesaid gentlemen have taken in the matter of originating or promoting the Lincoln Park project, a great deal, if not most of the credit is due to the old Board of Public Works, which came into existence in the year 1861. To prove this assertion it is only necessary to go back to the early reports of this body and to select from these the one submitted to the city council February 8th. 1862. Here Commissioners John G. Gindele (president of the Board for four years), Benjamin Carpenter and Frederick Letz make the following statement in reference to the old city cemetery:

Bridge in Lincoln Park.

" Perhaps as general an interest will be felt in the work done in that part of the grounds, lying north of the cemetery proper, and which has not yet been subdivided into lots. Here are some 40 acres of public grounds of diversified surface, bordering on the lake, covered with a young growth of wood, *and affording to the city the promise* of an attractive park, at a small expense. Without any large expenditure here, a good deal has been accomplished in giving the grounds an inviting appearance, and by trimming up and thinning the young trees, to secure a good growth and shape to such as are left standing. A gate has been built in this part of the grounds, and several small bridges thrown across the county ditch flowing through the grounds and discharging into the lake. Continuous drives will be made through the cemetery and *park, and the grounds made a pleasant place of resort for parties either walking or riding.* It is very desirable that these improvements should not be arrested here, and as the funds with which they have been made are nearly exhausted, that means be provided for their further progress."

And again, looking through the report of the Commissioners under date April 1, 1863, a year previous to the time Alderman Armstrong introduced his park ordinance to the council, we find the following pointed reference made to the desirability of establishing a park on the site where Lincoln Park now is situated: "But little could be done for the park, as the appropriation was very meagre. It would, doubtless, gratify the citizens to see well ornamented the small amount of public grounds which the city has. We especially recommend that liberal provisions be made for laying out and improving the grounds to be used for a park at the north of the cemetery. It is desirable that a regular plan be determined on for ornamenting these grounds, and for drives and walks connecting with the cemetery and connecting streets and that an annual appropriation be made to carry it out. This park will have an extent of about fifty acres."

This oasis in the busy metropolis of the west is situated only two miles distant from the Court House and is bounded on the east by Lake Michigan, on the north by Diversey Street, on the south by North Avenue and on the west by Clark Street. It is easily reached from the heart of the city by using the Clark or Wells Street Cable cars on their northward trips. Lincoln Park now contains over 300 acres, and is made all the more interesting through its many monuments of great and good men. The Park Board was created by an act of legislature in 1869, and four years later the condemnation proceedings were completed, the title to all the territory to be embraced within the parks except a small portion of the cemetery tract, acquired, and the Pine Street Drive was so far completed as to be opened for public use. In the original act E. B. McCagg, J. B. Turner, Joseph Stockton, Jacob Rehm and Andrew Nelson were named as the first Board of Commissioners. They met March 16, 1869, and were organized by the election of E. B. McCagg as President. The time of the Board for the first year was mainly devoted to a topographical study of the territory to be embraced within the Park—preparing plans for future improvements, and starting the machinery which had been devised by the law. On the 26th of February, 1871, the Board suffered a serious loss by the death of Mr. John B. Turner, one of its most valued members. By an act of the General Assembly approved June 16, 1871, provision was made for the appointment of a new Board of Commissioners, a question having been raised as to the power of the legislature to name the Commissioners in the law. In November, 1871, the Governor appointed as such Commissioners Samuel M. Nickerson, Joseph Stockton, Belden F. Culver, Wm. H. Bradley and Francis Kales, to succeed the Board which had been named in the original law. The first meeting of the new Board was held Nov. 28, 1871, and organized by the election of B. F. Culver as President. Under the administration of this Board proceedings were instituted for acquiring title to the various tracts of land embraced within the limits of the Park. In February, 1874, Commissioners Nickerson, Bradley and Kales resigned, and the Governor appointed as their successors, F. H. Winston, A. C. Hesing and Jacob Rehm. At the meeting of the Board Feb. 24, 1874, B. F. Culver resigned as President and F. H. Winston was elected as President of the Board.

During the term of this Board, the condemnation proceedings were completed. Commissioners Rehm and Hesing, who had done yeomen's service during the two years of their official labors and to whose indefatigable energy and foresight the Park Board of that time was deeply indebted, resigned in July 1876, and the Governor appointed as their successors, T. F. Withrow and L. J. Kadish. Commissioner Culver resigned in June, 1877, and the Governor appointed Max Hjortsberg as his successor.

Pursuant to the provisions of the original act, which contemplated, that Lincoln Park should be a City Park, the Board in 1869 applied to the Mayor of Chicago to issue the bonds of the city for an amount necessary for the purchase of the land to be embraced in the Park. The Mayor refusing to act in the matter, an application was made for a mandamus to compel the issue of the Bonds. The law being declared invalid, additional legislation became necessary, which by an act of the General Assembly approved June 16, 1871, authorized a special assessment to be made by the corporate authorities of the towns of North Chicago and Lake View (within which towns the Park lies), on all lands deemed benefitted, for the enlargement and improvement of Lincoln Park. Pursuant thereto, an assessment was made in 1873 and confirmed by the Circuit Court. On an appeal to the Supreme Court an error was pointed out in the law which again compelled the Commissioners to invoke the power of the Legislature, and ask that the law be amended in conformity with the decision of the Court.

A special assessment as provided by an act approved Feb. 18, 1874, was made in July, 1875, by the Supervisor and Assessor of the town of North Chicago on all lots and lands in said town deemed benefitted by the proposed improvement, and was sustained by the Supreme Court. Thus the Board had been enabled to secure the lands which are embraced within the limits of the Park. In the character of the improvements the various Boards have ever and successfully endeavored to keep the expenditures within their means, and have studiously avoided costly architectural display, preferring the simplest and most economical treatment consistent with good taste and the public requirements.

No Commissioner has at any time received any compensation for his services, nor have they derived any advantage, pecuniary or otherwise, from their connection with the Park Commission, except the pleasure realized from the public appreciation of their labors.

The southern portion of the park was formerly used by the city as a burying ground, and it became necessary of course to disinter the remains of those slumbering there and to remove them to Graceland and Rosehill Cemeteries.

Not one of our parks, with the exception perhaps of the much smaller Union Park, over on the West Side, is so near to the business centre of the city as Lincoln Park, to which fact it is chiefly due that it receives the lion's share of strangers coming to the city. The parks in other cities being less centrally located, and not so convenient of access, are frequented largely by the wealthier classes, the visitors in carriages far outnumbering those on foot. Lincoln Park, bordered on three sides by a dense population and convenient of approach, is the daily resort of all classes of the community, the poor as well as the rich enjoying the pleasure it affords; the pedestrians far outnumbering those who ride. Without any of the advantages of diversified surface, fertility of soil, or natural shade possessed by Parks elsewhere to aid in beautifying and improving the tract which the law has appropriated for the Park, there has been a constant struggle to reduce the soil (*if such the sandy surface may be termed*) to subjection, that the waste places might bloom. But it possesses also a number of attractive features, as yet lacking in the other parks of this city. To begin with, there is a very interesting and instructive zoological collection, then we have numerous monuments reared to statesmen, soldiers, men of letters, etc.; we can boast of an electric fountain of great splendour, a gift of Mr. Charles T. Yerkes, the President of the North and West Side Street Railway Companies, and last but not least, the refreshing, cool breezes, wafted over the shady walks and drives from the glittering waters of Lake Michigan.

The "Mall" in Lincoln Park.

But the most excellent feature, calling forth the admiration of the throngs of visitors promenading through the park during the summer time, is the gorgeous array of beautiful flowers extending north from the Schiller statue to the new palm house. Mr. Charles Stromback, the efficient and popular chief gardener of the park, is untiring in his efforts to please the public by showy and artistically arranged outdoor floral decorations. During the winter season he and his able staff of gardeners busy themselves with making ample provisions for the necessities of spring, when nature awakens to new life and activity. And then, when the tulips, hyacinths and other flowery messengers of spring have ceased to bloom, Mr. Stromback forthwith begins with the distribution of summer flowers, which he arranges along the magnificent expanse of lawns south of the palm house and elsewhere with praiseworthy skill and taste, whereupon he leaves it to kind mother earth and the sun's genial rays to carry his work to completion, to give the flowers further growth and enchanting beauty.

Here are to be seen the most lovely children of flora planted in long serpentine beds or in the shape of gaudy rugs and carpets. Of such carpet beds there are several that deserve close scrutiny on the part of the interested saunderer, as they are indeed to be classed among the best creations of artistic floriculture. The finest specimens may be found at both ends of the Bates fountain. Flowers in bewildering variety, velvety lawns, catalpa-trees, mighty vases and foliage plants, all combine to make the prospect one of rare beauty. Here it is where Mr. Stromback has used his skill to the best effect, and here it is where will be found many of the old favorites—pansies, geraniums, collodium, verbenas, heliotrope, pinks, single chrysanthemum, linum grandiflorum, gilliflowers, gladiolus, roses, larkspur, cock's-comb, daisies, balsam, petunia's, etc. Following the winding path we come to the aforesaid Bates fountain which forms the centre of this floral exhibition. It was presented to the people of Chicago by the lamented philanthropist, Eli Bates, and may be described as follows: In a circular basin, walled with granite, sportive boys—half fish, half human—are frolicking. Graceful swans join in the sport and shower water over the laughing youngsters and their finny prizes. In the center rises a clump of bulrushes with their slender, graceful leaves. The design is harmonious—it is the work of Augustus St. Gaudens—and of merit. South of the fountain, at the southern boundary of the flower garden, stands the famous figure of Germany's great poet, Friedrich Schiller. This fine monument was donated to the park and the people by the German-American citizens of Chicago through one of their leading associations—the Swabian Society. The statue is a noble work and well exemplifies the greatness of the German thinker and writer.

The unveiling of this monument took place on Saturday, May 15, 1886. Originally the ninth day of May, the anniversary of Schiller's death, had been decided upon as the date for the unveiling ceremonies, but the excitement prevailing at that time among all classes of our population, in consequence of the anarchistic bomb throwing at the Haymarket, made a postponement imperatively necessary. Notwithstanding the inclemency of the weather on May 15, the Germans of Chicago and vicinity turned out in great masses to do honor to the occasion and to participate in the dedicatory exercises in Lincoln Park, where the large throng, sheltered under an extensive black roof of open umbrellas, patiently listened to the able speeches and the soul-inspiring songs of the united German singing societies. The oration of the day was delivered by Mr. Wilhelm Rapp, Editor in chief of the Illinois Staats Zeitung; the other speakers were Carter H. Harrison, then Mayor of Chicago, and Mr. Julius Rosenthal, Chairman of the Monument Committee.

The Swabian Society started the movement that led to the erection of this monument in the month of November, 1880, and nearly four years later, on September 1, 1884, a committee of German Citizens was appointed for the purpose of collecting the funds needed to complete the sum that was necessary to pay for the monument and to carry to a successful termination the noble work begun by the Swabian Society. On January 1, 1884, there were on hand already $5.022 for this purpose, and it did not take the committee a very long time to bring the enterprise to a highly satisfactory issue. The Committee consisted of the following well known Germans: Franz Amberg, August Bauer, Franz Demmler, Hermann De Vry, Emil Dietzsch, Edward S. Dreyer, Joseph Frank, Carl Haerting, C. E. Heiss, Phil. Henne, A. C. Hesing, Arnold Holinger, Louis Huck, Theodor Karls, Francis Lackner, Andrew C. Leicht, T J Lefens, Leopold Mayer, Fridolin Madlener, C. C. Möller, Louis Nettelhorst, Georg Prüssing, Julius Rosenthal, Harry Rubens, Dr. Rudolph Seiffert, Max Stern, Gustav Stieglitz, Jos. Schöninger, Frank Wenter, Geo. A. Weiss and Ludwig Wolff.

The corner stone of the foundation was laid on Nov. 11, 1885, and six months later the statue formed one of the grandest and most interesting sights in Lincoln Park. It was cast by Wm. Pelargus, of Stuttgart, Germany, and is an exact copy of the Schiller statue in Marbach, which was cast from a bust modelled from life by the celebrated sculptor Dannecker. The chief excellence of the Schiller statue in Lincoln Park is found in its wonderful artistic simplicity. It is 10 feet high and must be seen to be appreciated. The unveiling ceremonies were very impressive, notwithstanding the rain and were witnessed by over 10,000 people, among which were no less than sixty different German societies and lodges. After the exercises in the open air and rain had been concluded, a banquet took place in the Refectory, where more speeches were delivered and where the celebrated German Gemuethlichkeit reigned supreme.

North of the palm house stands the colossal figure of Linnaeus, which was presented to the park by the countrymen of the great botanist and was unveiled May 23, 1891. The first actual step was taken when the Linnean Monument Association was organized and incorporated. An executive committee of 45 persons was appointed at the same time. This committee issued a call to the Swedes of America asking for contributions, but as the responses were few and far between, it soon became apparent that the Swedish residents of Chicago had either to abandon the project or perform the task themselves unaided by outsiders. The greater part of the funds expended has consequently been raised in this city, partly by liberal subscriptions and partly through picnics and other public entertainments, in which the secular Swedish societies have shown much interest by making considerable contributions in the way of patronage. The first president of the monument association was Mr. J. A. Enander, who was succeeded by Mr. Robert Lindblom, to whose pluck and push a good deal of the early success must be ascribed. The monument is a very creditable work of art. The model was made by C. J. Dufverman in Stockholm, where, too, the statue was cast by Otto Meyer and Co. The cost of the whole, as it now stands on a pedestal of granite shipped from Maine is $15,000. But there are to be added four figures representing as many different sciences, viz.: botany, medicine, chemistry and zoology, in all of which Linne had extensive knowledge. When thus finished there will have been expended about $22,000. These allegorical figures will, it is expected, be ready and put in their proper places within a very short time. The statue is 39 feet high from the base to the apex. The height of the figure is 14½ feet. When complete, the monument will be an exact counterpart of the Linne monument erected in Stockholm some years ago.

Those of the Directors of the Monument Association, who deserve special mention for liberality in cash contributions and untiring efforts during the four years that elapsed since the work was commenced are—Robert Lindblom, Andrew Chaiser, P. S. Peterson, L. G. Hallberg, C. O. Carlson, F. A. Lindstrand, A. E. Johnson, Nils Anderson, August Jernberg, Victor Rylander, Lawrence Hesselroth, O. F Vidman, Chas. Eklund, Alexander J. Johnson and many others.

The unveiling ceremonies were preceded by a large procession. The presentation speech was delivered by Mr. Robert Lindblom and the speech of acceptance by the President of the Lincoln Park Board. Mayor Washburne followed with a few remarks and then gave way to Mr. C. F. Peterson, who recited a poem written for the occasion. The orator of the day was Mr. John A. Enander, who spoke in Swedish. After the conclusion of the dedication

Schiller Statue in Lincoln Park.

ceremonies the vast throng adjourned to Thielemann's summer resort just outside the northern boundaries of the Park, where the celebration of the day was continued. Among those who spoke there were Robert Lindblom, C. F. Peterson, Rev. H. Lindskog and Dr. Frithjof Larson. As Secretary of the Monument Association, Mr. Lawrence Hesselroth has rendered valuable services, and so has Mr. Louis Widestrand in the capacity of Financial Secretary. Others who have displayed much enthusiasm and sacrificed time and money in the enterprise are L. F. Hussander, Richard Lindgren, Nils Anderson, Gustave Svenson, Chas. Stromback, head gardener of Lincoln Park, P. A. Sundelius, S. A. Freeman, and many more.

At the southern end of the park the statue of the great and good Abraham Lincoln is the dominant attraction. The surroundings of this monumental work seem to have been arranged with no other object than to embrace its beauties. It faces North Avenue and is approached by a winding drive which circles from both the Clark Street and the Lake Shore Drive entrances. A concourse is placed before it where carriages can assemble, while the occupants view the figure of the great emancipator at their leisure. Augustus St. Gaudens was the sculptor. The cost of this great work was about $40,000. The late Eli Bates presented it to the park, and the expense was borne by his estate.

Among the other monuments which adorn this lovely park, the equestrian statue of General Grant attracts the most attention. The demonstration attending the formal dedication of this monument October 7, 1891, was a very imposing affair and the exercises throughout were of a character thoroughly in keeping with the dignity of the occasion. The parade and the naval display off Lincoln Park were witnessed by many thousands of people, and the oratory, which was heard by comparatively few of the great multitudes that were out for the day, was of a character to command attention and respect. Judge Gresham's tribute to the old commander was comprehensive, appreciative and in entire good taste, while the other speakers performed the duties assigned to them in a manner that left nothing to be desired.

The monument to Grant was designed for the soldiers of the army whose tattered flags fluttered about the pedestal on that memorable day. The face that looked over the troubled flood of Lake Michigan as the descending sun broke from the clouds and painted the dancing waters, was not the face of Grant in his later and weaker hours. But it was the face the veterans had seen years ago when trudging over the dusty roads of Tennessee and Virginia, when they turned to cheer the iron man who was to lead them to victory. He sat then as the bronze sits now, firmly astride his horse, plain almost to a point of affectation in his dress—the army coat that covered his sturdy frame as threadbare as theirs, the worn slouched hat a rebuke to the frippery of the staff. His face in the statue is the face of that day—a firm and dogged face; the eyes intent under the gathered brow as if watching the smoke of the skirmish lines, the lips compressed, the firmness of the jaw showing through the rough beard.

Something of affectation for Grant, who sprang from the good soil of northern Illinois; something of pride in the fact that Chicago was first of the great towns of America to unveil a fit monument to the hero, and something of the popular love of holiday parades and bands, combined to choke the streets along the lake with the greatest crowd in memory. It was not only Chicago—although more than half the town turned out to block the line of march and surge across the meadows of Lincoln Park—but from early morning crowded trains drew to the city the population of the suburbs for hundreds of miles. They were the preliminary shower that was afterwards lost in the downpour when the floodgates of the city were loosened.

More than two hundred thousand people lined Michigan Avenue and the cross streets from Park Row to the river to see the great pageant, unquestionably the popular feature of the Grant Memorial Day. Neither rain nor mud deferred the vast crowd from standing for fully four hours wedged in the jam such as only Chicago and the much abused and yet famous lake front can produce. Along the east side of the regatta course in Lincoln Park, for nearly half a mile, and in the meadow that lies about the monument, 500,000 people

2

had gathered. On the banks of the boat course they sat in tiers as about an amphitheatre, making a foreground of changing line—as the mass of faces turned in the sunlight—for the fleet bobbing at anchor in the surge. The roughness of the day prevented a great naval display, but the revenue cutters and steamers, flaming with the colors at their yards, and rising, falling and swinging with the swell, were impressive. It is not given to the widow of every soldier or statesman, however great he may have been, to witness hundreds of thousands assembled to do homage to the memory of a loved husband. It was a wondrous sight that met the gaze of Mrs. Grant as she drove out from the residence of Potter Palmer to take her place in the fourth division of the procession as the most distinguished of the goodly army of distinguished guests. Dressed in black and wearing glasses, Mrs. Grant looked highly pleased at the warm reception she received from the assembled thousands. Drawn by two handsome roans and with the coachman and footman in livery, Potter Palmer's carriage took up its position on the right of the leading four carriages of the division. Alongside Mrs. Grant was seated the popular President of the Board of Lady Managers of the World's Fair, Mrs. Potter Palmer, looking radiant and pleased at the reception given her honored guest. In the carriage also were Ulysses Grant and Potter Palmer. All along the route Mrs. Grant was warmly cheered and she responded by bowing and smiling.

Mr. Edward S. Dreyer, the well-known German-American banker, Ex-President of the Real Estate Board of Chicago, and at that time also Chairman of the Board of Trustees of the Grant Monument Association, had the high honor conferred upon him to preside over this gigantic meeting. He opened the ceremonies with a neat little speech, and then introduced Rev. Bishop Newman, who invoked divine blessing on the day's undertaking and the people assembled. The principal oration was delivered by Judge Gresham, while shorter speeches were made by Mr. Edward S. Taylor, the popular Secretary of the Board of Lincoln Park Commissioners and Mayor Washburne.

As the last speaker stepped from the stand Chairman Dreyer declared that the exercises were over. But he raised his hand as the people began to move away and introduced Louis F. Rebisso, the sculptor, who threw all the strength of his genius into the statue which now stands for aye in Lincoln Park. The old soldiers cheered heartily for the man who had moulded the form of their loved general. Cries for a speech from the sculptor made those turn back who were going away. But Mr. Rebisso shook his head and declined to speak.

Two hours after the death of General U. S. Grant, July 23, 1885, Potter Palmer had subscribed $5,000 to a monument fund, and before the evening of the fourth day after the General's death nearly $42,000 had been raised. This was the remarkable beginning of one of the most spontaneous and popular memorials ever offered by a people. While New York rode up the Hudson drive to a vacant knoll where Grant's monument was to have overlooked the great river bend, the people of Chicago were gathered around the largest and finest bronze statue of the kind ever cast in America, commemorating with uncovered heads the life of that greatest of soldier statesmen.

At no time in the history of the statue association was there the slightest difficulty in securing subscriptions. A committee of citizens were selected to receive moneys in various ways and from the different classes, industries and societies of the city. This committee was as follows:

Henry Towner,	Jacob Grommes,	S. B. Raymond,
J. D. Harvey,	T. J. Lefens,	M. Selz,
Norman Williams,	H. W. Fuller,	Joseph Charles,
George H. Rozet,	C. Henrotin,	Edward Rose,
Thomas F. Cunningham,	George Schmidt,	John Grosse,
C. B. Farwell,	Robert Lindblom,	Charles Kern,
J. T. McAuley,	E. F. Cragin,	Charles H. Wacker,
W. T. Johnson,	S. N. Jewett,	J. B. Sullivan,
Louis Wampold,	P. E. Stanley,	M. Schweisthal.
Henry Wieland,	P. P. Heywood,	

Another committee was created as a board of trustees and to oversee the

The Linné Monument in Lincoln Park.

1559

designing and erecting of the memorial. **This committee** or board was chosen as follows:

E. S. Dreyer,	J. McGregor Adams,	Samuel M. Nickerson,
William E. Strong,	Norman Williams,	Joseph Stockton.
Potter Palmer,	Edward S. Taylor,	

When the fund was complete it amounted to about $65,000. Many different memorials were advocated before the committee, and it was only after long discussion that the present base and statue were decided upon. General Schofield wished a simple figure of Grant, supporting his desire by the homely and noble sentiment, that Grant needed no compliment. Mr. Rebisso, the sculptor, made first a drawing and then a model before his design for a figure was accepted. Had not Mr. Rebisso been ill for nearly a year and the first casting by M. M. Mossman, of Chicopee, Mass., been defective, the work would have been finished long before.

The statue combines grace and grandeur. It has force and solidity. The pedestal and base of Hallowell granite are majestic. This foundation was designed by F. M. Whitehouse of Chicago. Mr. Rebisso modeled the general sitting finely and easily in the saddle, holding the reins in the left hand and grasping a field glass in the right. The right hand is lowered to the thigh and the pose of the body suggests a careful survey of the field. The purpose is to convey Grant's concentration of mind; his confidence in fortune, his officers and men, and his own self reliance. It is 18 feet and 3 inches from the bottom of the plinth to the crown of the slouch hat. The location of the statue was chosen out of regard for popular sentiment. The larger subscribers preferred to have it stand in the northern section, but when they discovered that the people preferred it to stand on the lake shore near the southern end, the larger subscribers at once submitted.

Then there was erected a few years ago a life-size statue to the explorer, Robert La Salle. It was donated by Hon. Lambert Tree and was designed by De La Laing, a noted Belgian Sculptor. And on a hill located between the lower park lake and the Lake Shore Drive is the celebrated Ryerson monument, an Indian group in bronze. The figures are those of an Indian, with his wife, child and dog, on the alert, as if watching the approach of a stranger, not yet declared a foe, but still too remote to give assurance of friendly design. The pedestal which supports this group is in complete harmony with the bronze. Panels descriptive of various phases of Indian life are attached to the square support on which the group rests. The whole effect is realistic in the extreme. On the pedestal is the following inscription:

TO THE

OTTAWA NATION OF INDIANS,

MY EARLY FRIENDS,

PRESENTED BY MARTIN RYERSON.

Samuel Johnston, a well-known Chicagoan, who died a few years ago, left instructions to his executors to expend $10,000 for a statue of Shakespeare to be placed in the park.

East of the imposing palm house, on a hill, are located the greenhouses. Here the work of propagating the hundreds of thousands of bedding plants that are to decorate the park in the summer months goes on "while nights are dark and snows are white." Here are designed the plans for ornamental beds. The greenhouse is of course under the supervision of Mr. C. Stromback. His work is important, surely. He has able competitors in the various parks of the other divisions of the city, and to see to it that Lincoln Park does not lag behind in the race for floral excellence, keeps his brain and his hands busy. All the buildings are connected and under one roof—if the conventional affair of iron and glass that covers a conservatory can be properly designated as such. The propagating houses describe themselves in their name. Here are found countless foliage plants in little pots, duplicated from one another, as they outgrow their limits, and constantly increasing in number. The household favorites are here—all of them, as well as the varieties peculiar for their oddity as well as beauty.

Besides all this wealth and beauty of flowers, which must be seen to be appreciated, Lincoln Park has to offer another rare attraction upon its floral domain, namely, two lily ponds. These are situated in the eastern portion of the park, north of the waterworks, and they form, in a decidedly prominent degree, an object of genuine and unstinted admiration. This feature is a welcome novelty and deserves the highest praise.

Excepting in New York, no attempt has been made in public parks of this country outside of Chicago to display with fullness the strange beauty of the gorgeous specimens of lilies, that make the rivers and pools of the tropics their home. Everyone has heard of the Victoria Regia, or Amazon lily, the leaves of which are six feet in diameter, with blossoms fourteen inches wide. But not everyone has seen a specimen of this giant lily.

The lily basins have been constructed after the most approved plans. Warmth, shelter from high winds, and sunshine are necessary to ensure success. These requisites have been found in the little valley in which the pools are located. A bird's-eye view of the two pools, when stocked and with their plants in bloom, will furnish a pleasure to which the western sense is unused.

There are numerous specimens of the genus Nymphaea represented, the most celebrated of which unquestionably is the Victoria Regia. This great lily, if properly protected, can be grown and flowered in the open air. When first open, the flowers are pure white and produce an odor of rare fragrance, which can best be compared to the flavor of the pineapple. After the first night the flowers change to a pink tint, lose their fragrance, and after living through another day they slowly sink into the water, there to ripen their seed. A new variety of the Victoria Regia, of which a specimen will doubtless be obtained, is crimson flowered. This plant is more robust than the white flowered Victoria, and the young leaves are of a dark bronze color. The flowers of this new variety are white on the day of opening, but change to a dark crimson color later.

The night-blooming water lilies—seven kinds—open their flowers after dark, beginning at about six o'clock and remaining expanded until about the same time next morning. The flowers appear on stalks elevated ten or twelve inches above the surface of the water. The Nymphæa Devoniensis is one of the choicest of the night-blooming lilies. In one season a single plant will cover a circle twenty feet across, with leaves twenty-five inches in diameter and flowers that are a foot from tip to tip of petals. The Nymphæa Devoniensis can be successfully dwarfed, if it is desired. The leaves are green with serrated edges. The blossoms, rose red with scarlet stamens, appear to great advantage by artificial light. We see here the Nymphæa Tuberosa and the Odorata Rosa, whose home is in North America; the lotus plants are of Egyptian origin, the Nymphaea Candidissima is of English origin, the Flava came from Florida, the dwarf water lily from China, the N. Devoniensis from India, the Zanzibarensis and Dentata from Africa. The N. Sturtevanti, a new semi-double, red water lily, is a very fine plant. Its foliage is of a light bronze color, approaching crimson. The N. Rubra is also a native of India and it somewhat resembles the N. Devoniensis.

It must not be supposed that all the beauties of the lily ponds, with their abundance of glorious water plants, can be seen at one visit. Frequent trips must be made, including night excursions, when electric lights will shed their lustre on the night blooming lilies. Many other plants besides water lilies are grown in and around the ponds. Water Hyacinths, Sagittarias, ornamental rushes and grasses, with the curious floating Stratoitis and other interesting forms of plant life, fill up the spaces not covered by the shield-like leaves of the Nymphaea's, making altogether a grand display either by day or under the electric lights.

Another delightful spot is the "mall," north of the Lincoln monument, which extends for a quarter of a mile in a northerly direction and terminates in the lower artificial park lake. Here the pedestrian rules supreme. Bordered with beds of flowers, beyond which extend lawns of velvety softness, the

Lincoln Park.—Flower-Parterre, showing Old Palm House.

mall offers as enjoyable a promenade as could be wished. Here, as in the space between the greenhouses and the Schiller statue, the gardener's art is seen at its best. Carefully trimmed and well cared for beds of flowers lend color to the view as they shed fragrance abroad. Viewed from the mall, the lower lake presents on a bright summer day an animated scene. Pleasure boats ply here and there, laden with happy oarsmen and their friends. The Swans have chosen for their home an island in the lower lake. Their graceful forms, as they float about in the water, are a pleasure to the eye.

Before we turn away from the floral displays of Mr. Stromback to other spots of interest and delight, we will take a walk through the palm house just lately finished. This floral palace has, with the exception of the horticultural hall at the World's Fair grounds, no peer in this entire land of ours. It is of imposing dimensions, with its mighty arched glass roof and its gigantic proportions throughout. The palm house proper is 156 feet long and 90 feet wide; its height is 50 feet. The conservatory, connected with the main building, is 96 feet long, 31 feet wide and 21 feet high, and the other addition, extending north from the palm house proper, giving shelter to a rare collection of orchids, measures 100 feet in length and 30 feet in width. To this complex of buildings another, a fernery, was added at the northeast corner. With the exception of the foundation walls, none of these buildings contain any other material than glass and steel, so that the light of day has full sway.

In the heating of this fine building some comparatively new features are introduced. The hot water method has been adopted, radiating coils of one and a quarter inch pipes will be concealed in chambers behind rock work. The radiating pipe service is arranged in independent sections and each section controlled by an automatic heat regulating device. The boilers being distant from the palm house about 350 feet, leave the palm house range in its beautiful lines clear from suggestion of shed or factory. The floor grade of the house is established at a point six and one-half feet above the lawn surface. Broad terraces surround the building on three sides. The front terraces command a good view of the flower garden, a broad handsome walk and stairways lead the visitor from the flower garden up the slopes of the terraces to the front entrance of the palm house; the plants are arranged in natural positions, branches, flower pots and tubs are banished. A winding path leads round a rocky point, then again across an open space, every turn revealing some new beauty, while from certain points the whole may be taken in at a general view. By planting out in the soil bed greater luxuriance of growth will be obtained, the plants will the sooner produce an effect proportional to the magnificence of their home. Harmonious arrangements of rocks were introduced to give character to the surface of the soil. Tall palms, cycads, tree-ferns and bamboos rear aloft their heads, while below are seen the shade loving ferns, mosses and other beautiful forms of plant life, and from truss and column hang climbers of many kinds, some of beautiful foliage, and others covered with flowers, twining among the iron of the structure and covering it with a luxuriant tropical growth, blending the whole into a natural grouping of Nature's loveliest forms.

The conservatory will be used for exhibition of plants from temperate climes, or of plants of beautiful foliage or graceful habit of growth, requiring temperate conditions of heat. The fernery is striking and effective in some of its features; the design for the interior takes the form of a rocky dell with a glass roof. A cascade was introduced, the water tumbling from rock to rock into a pool at the bottom, while on ledges, in fissures, or on the faces of the moss covered rocks, are planted the various beautiful forms of the fern family.

And now we will take a glance at some of the most important improvements accomplished within the last few years, namely the extensive work along the lake shore, consisting of nothing less than the building of a sea wall and beach, which has been carried forward under the efficient supervision of the park Superintendent, J. A. Pettigrew. This improvement became necessary to protect the shore along the park against the inroads of Lake Michigan. The Fitz Simons and Connell Company, in 1874, built the first substantial breakwater, commencing at Oak Street and running to North Avenue. Upon this structure, cut down (at the suggestion of General Fitz Simons to Commissioner Adams in 1886), the present sea wall was built. The breakwater running north from North Avenue, the present new beach improvement, was constructed by the above named firm in conjunction with the Green Dredging Co. and the Chicago Dredging and Dock Co.

Commencing with a breakwater at Bellevue Place and running northward, a large tract was taken from Lake Michigan, making possible the extension of the Lake Shore Drive south to Oak Street; at North Ave. the scope of the work was extended, the breakwater was curved further out into the lake, until the plan as at present outlined, embraces on a frontage included within the park the reclamation from Lake Michigan of about 140 acres.

In 1886 the work of construction of the sea wall began, according to the plans of Major T. H. Handbury, Engineer Corps, U. S. A. The piling of the breakwater was sawn off below water line, a platform of three inch oak plank was laid across from front to back, and the work of casting the huge blocks of concrete commenced; the magnificent blocks, each weighing nearly ten tons, and formed out of the "Germania" brand of Portland cement, were added one to the other, until in the fall of 1888 there stood on the breakwater an unbroken line (extending from Bellevue to Burton Place), 2,889 feet long and 10 feet high, presenting a massive front to the storms of Lake Michigan.

The paved beach work commences at North Ave. and is constructed from designs by Capt. W. H. Marshall, Engineer Corps, U. S. A.; excepting the dredging and pile driving, all the work has been done by park employees. The breakwater facing this improvement seaward is constructed of two rows of close pile work, 10 feet in width from outside to outside. The lakeward row is faced to landward with close 3 inch oak-sheeting bolted to a 12x4 oak wale, and the landward side of the landward row of piles faced landward with Wakefield patent sheet piling, the breakwater being filled with stone and sawn off to a point 10 inches above lake level. Landward from the breakwater rises the paved beach 48 feet wide, rising 1 foot in 8, then rising by two steps of one foot each to a promenade of 16 feet in width, which is further flanked on the landward side by a parapet of two steps rising from each side, the base being four feet six inches wide and the top two feet wide; landward of the promenade and parallel with it is a driveway 45 feet in width, and from thence to the inner lake or rowing course a sloping turf-covered bank planted with trees and shrubs. The character of the work is of the most substantial description, the pavement of the beach being composed of granite blocks eight inches in depth, laid on a bed of concrete six inches in depth, while the joints are run with Portland cement grouting. The promenade and parapets are of the finest grade of granite beton on Portland cement concrete base. The driveway is granite faced with granite block and granite beton curbs and gutters. For connection across the inlet a swing or drawbridge was built, so that after converting Fullerton Ave. pier into a bridge connecting with the park, the drive from North Ave. along the beach to the park at Fullerton Ave. becomes continuous and uninterrupted.

The zoological garden forms one of the most attractive features the park possesses, and the mecca during each returning season of many thousands of children and adults. At the present writing it numbers among its numerous inhabitants the following: 2 African lions, 1 flying fox, 5 monkeys, 2 tigers, 2 leopards, 5 pumas, 2 wild cats, 1 lynx, 3 wolf-hounds, 2 wolfs, 22 foxes, 1 ferret, 1 wild-cat, 4 badgers, 1 otter, 13 bears, among which are 2 brown, 7 black, 2 grey and 2 cinnamon-colored, 12 coons, 143 squirrels, 4 opossums, 1 sea-lion, 22 white rats, 5 beavers, 2 porcupines, 10 wood-cocks, 20 guinea-pigs, 24 rabbits and hares, 50 prairie dogs, 10 buffaloes, 1 wild goat, 15 cashmere goats, 7 mooses or elks, 1 fallow-deer, 11 Virginia roes, 1 lama, 1 elephant, 1 elk, 1 jaguar, 1 Turkish eagle, 17 eagles, 7 buzzards, 18 owls, 3 magpies, 4 parrots, 3 cockatoos, 12 ring-doves, 19 peacocks, 3 pheasants, 4 quails, 2 cranes, 3 hawks, 11 white geese, 7 white swans, 3 pelicans, 20 turtles, 15 crocodiles, 2 lizards, 3 rattle snakes and 1 land turtle.

During the Spring of 1878 the Board converted the pier at North Avenue to the uses of a Floating Hospital; constructing proper guards and appropriate

Indian Group in Lincoln Park.

shelter for little children. Upwards of five thousand ailing children visited this resort annually and found health in the refreshing breezes from the lake. In some instances mothers have come with their babes at sunrise and tarried all day. A steamer made regular trips between the city and the pier during the season. Medical attendance, competent nurses and pure milk were furnished by the Floating Hospital Association. This floating hospital was abandoned some years ago, but since that time a much larger and more useful one has been established by the managers of the "Daily News" Fresh Air Fund. This sanitarium can be found near the lake shore at the foot of Belden Avenue. The present Commissioners of Lincoln Park are: Wm. C. Goudy, President; Charles S. Kirk, John V. Clark, jr., R. A. Waller and August Heuer; E. S. Taylor, is the Secretary and C. J. Blair, Treasurer.

New Palm House in Lincoln Park.

THE SOUTH PARK SYSTEM.

In the year 1865 there was some talk of establishing a public Park somewhere in the South Division of Chicago, but the proposition did not assume definite shape till the Autumn of 1866. Prior to the meeting of the General Assembly several meetings were held at which the question was discussed. It was thought advisable to make the effort. The City had no old Cemetery to donate, and the land for the Park would have to be purchased outright. The gentlemen most prominent at that time in the agitation of the question were Thomas Hoyne, Governor William Bross, J. Y. Scammon, H. H. Honoré, Paul Cornell, J. Irving Pierce, L. B. Sidway, Chauncey T. Bowen, Judge John M. Wilson, John D. Jennings.

Governor Bross was very enthusiastic about it. He had made the acquaintance of Fred Law Olmsted, the great American landscape artist, who had made a wonderful success of Central Park, New York, and the "Deacon", as he was then called infused much sentiment into the scheme. There was a beautiful tract of land known as Egandale, lying west of Cottage Grove Avenue, and north of 55th St. which through the sentiment and enterprise of the late Dr. William B. Egan had become almost a perfected Park. It was planted abundantly with evergreens and other trees, was laid out with beautiful drives and in a general way was looked upon by the public as a desirable "catch" for Park purposes. Ezra B. McCagg, partner of Mr. Scammon, prepared a bill for the establishment of a Park, which substantially absorbed "Egandale." The 25th General Assembly convened in January, 1867, and the bill was duly introduced. But opposition was manifested at once. The estate of Dr. Egan had by foreclosures, substantially passed into the control of the Smith's of Chicago and the Drexel's of Philadelphia, and accordingly there appeared on the scene as representatives of those interested; Mr. Norman Williams and Mr. Norman C. Perkins, gentlemen well selected to protect their clients' interests. The Egandale interests wanted a Park, but wanted no part of Egandale taken. They wanted Egandale to front on the Park, all around, or on as many sides as possible. The outsiders did not want *their* land taken, but were very desirous Egandale should be, for as they said, it was already a Park. The general public looked on with various degrees of interest. Some favored Egandale, some opposed any park scheme. Some said Egandale was too far away from the city (!) The Press expressed all kinds of opinions—there were many battles fought, all harmless, but there was sufficient confusion and quarreling to bring matters to a dead-lock. At last a conference was held at the Leland House one Saturday evening. It was a circus. Besides the curious lookers-on, there were present Chauncey Bowen, S. S. Hayes, H. H. Honoré, James P. Root, Gen. George W Smith, Gov. Bross, Melville W. Fuller, J. Irving Pierce, Norman C. Perkins, Norman Williams, J. K. C. Forrest, Paul Cornell, John C. Dore and Frank Eastman, both senators, the members of the House from the south side, and others whose names do not now occur to the writer. It was a stormy meeting. Everybody tried to be wise and amiable, and everybody had a mad fit. At last the bill was passed around for amendment and a compromise was affected. Egandale consented to the taking of a strip from the west side along Cottage Grove Avenue, and a strip from the south side along 55th street. It was deemed advisable to get to the lake, so it was agreed that there should be a strip to Lake Michigan. Mr. Root agreed to the arrangement provided he could locate the south line of the strip, which he did as it gave him three hundred feet front on the strip. Others fixed lines with reference to their own property, and everybody became hilariously happy—the whole matter was referred to George W Smith and James P. Root, to prepare a satisfactory bill. No one ever saw the bill after it left their hands until it was introduced in the legislature. The account of that meeting was written by Mr Forrest, and by Melville W Fuller, which ap-

Grant Monument in Lincoln Park.

peared in the "Chicago Times" the following Monday. While the authors of the report adhered to the fact, they let nothing of a Pickwickian character escape them. The Bill became a law. It was required to be submitted to the people at the annual Town Meeting in South Chicago, Hyde Park and Lake. Many of the people who had not been educated up to a high appreciation of the benefits of a grand Park, voted against it, and were joined by others who thought the whole thing was a real estate steal. The election was close, and the scheme probably carried in fact, but by reason of some confusion as to the ballot the result was declared against the Park. Mr. Thomas Hoyne, then an earnest advocate of a park system, contested the matter in the Courts, but the result finally was a miscarriage.

In 1868, the question of a park was again agitated. The same gentlemen and others interested met often, sometimes in secret, and once in a while in public. The matter was discussed in every real estate office in Chicago. All kinds of parks were marked out on the maps. The papers would announce that a park had been agreed on, and when the public became advised of the location, a howl would go up all along the line. The promoters of the park, however, substantially agreed on the location, and the ground was designated in the act, which was prepared by Judge Beckwith. About the time the General Assembly convened, the question was discussed as to who should introduce the Bill. As the park was on the south side, it was appropriate that it should be a south side member, and as the land was nearly, if not all, in Mr. Francis Munson's district, he was selected. There was no particular opposition to the bill. James P. Root was Clerk of the House, and he saw to it, that there was no unnecessary delay. It passed, became a law, was submitted to the people, and carried by a good substantial majority.

No one person has ever claimed to be the discoverer of the South Park system, but each has ever been ready to accord to the other his full mend of praise.

The West and North sides were out in force looking after their park interests, and when the General Assembly adjourned, three park systems were provided for. At the same session (1869) the "Lake Front" Bill was introduced. The public is too well advised of its purport to give here any details concerning it, but it may be well to consider, what connection there was between the park bills and the lake front bill.

As has been seen, the park interests from the three divisions of the city were in Springfield in force. They had prearranged their various interests, and of course were patent factors in the matter of legislation. The promoters of the lake front interest understood this very well, and either to secure the co-operation of the Park interest, or at least not to antagonize it, shrewdly provided that, when what remained as the property of the city after the Illinois Central Co. had taken what it wanted, should be sold, the proceeds should be divided among the several parks in proportion to the assessed value of property in the respective divisions of the city. The lake front bill became a law, and its subsequent history is known to all. None of the parks ever derived any benefit from it.

By the way, the land was not purchased any too soon, for at present prices a park would have been impossible. Some of the prices at the time seemed extravagant. By the push, the enterprise, the public spirit of Chicago's citizens, we have an estate, whose value financially, aesthetically and sanitarily can never be estimated.

The selection of these lands was made within the time specified by the act establishing the South Park. Immediately thereafter the lands were examined and diligent inquiry was made in relation to their value. The probable cost of the lands was estimated at $1,865,740 and an application was made to the Circuit Court for the appointment of three assessors to assess the amount upon the property benefited. This application was refused and then the Supreme Court was asked for a mandamus, which was granted. Thereupon the Circuit Court appointed assessors who entered, immediately, upon the performance of their duties. About this time a nursery was established containing about five acres and over 60,000 trees, from 1 to 4 inches in diameter, were set out. They consisted of Maple, Elm, Sycamore,

Beach. Butternut, Cherry, Balsam, Linden, Ash, Birch, Arbor Vitæ, Pine and Hemlock and besides these there were purchased over 6,000 choice Evergreens from three to seven feet high. This nursery for the future supply of trees and shrubs and the work performed therein proved very interesting to many of the visitors and for that reason it was made accessible to the public, but it is now a thing of the past, for it had to make room for the World's Fair Buildings along Midway Plaisance, and only a small portion of this tree school could be preserved.

The South Park system embraces the World's Fair site and contains much more territory than all the other parks put together. Like the Commissions of Lincoln Park and the West Parks, the Board of South Park Commissioners was organized in 1869, by authority of an act of the Legislature, approved April 16th, of that year.

To defray the cost of acquiring the private property within the limits named in the act, a special assessment was levied upon all real property in the South Town of Chicago, Village of Hyde Park and Town of Lake, proportioned according to benefits to the property on account of the location of the Parks and Boulevards. The assessment was divided into eight annual installments. For improvement and maintenance an annual levy is made upon all property assessed in the three towns named, which is collected with the annual State and County Tax.

The management of the Parks is vested in five Commissioners appointed by the judges of the Circuit Court of Cook County; the term of office is five years, one Commissioner being appointed each year. The Commissioners constitute a municipal corporation, having exclusive jurisdiction over the Parks and Boulevards.

In April 1869 Governor Palmer appointed as Commissioners the following gentlemen : John M. Wilson, George W. Gage, Chauncey T. Bowen, L. B. Sidway and Paul Cornell. This Commission commenced its labors by selecting the land designated by the act and the cost of which was at first estimated at $1,865,750. After the appointment of assessors, however, it was found that the land required would cost a sum much larger than the original estimate. Thereupon it was decided to increase the assessment to $3,320,-000, and to issue bonds for the full amount of $2,000,000. The majority of the bonds were sold in New York and from them together with those that were used in part payment for the acquired land, the Board realized $1,827,399.

In 1869 the landscape gardeners Olmstead & Vaux, of New York, were employed to furnish plans and specifications for improvement of the park grounds. Then work was begun in earnest and carried on with great vigor, when the great fire of 1871 put a stop to the operations. The headquarters of the Commission were burned and with them all the original plans and specifications, the records, atlases of the towns of Hyde Park and Lake, vouchers, contracts, estimates, assessment rolls, etc. Actual work had, however, progressed too far to allow a long interruption of the undertaking. In the year following new boulevards were laid out and graded, and in September 1872 H. W. S. Cleveland was appointed landscape gardener. To the plans furnished by Messrs. Olmstead & Vaux there was this objection raised, that the expense of constructing the Parks and Boulevards in the manner they had indicated, would involve an outlay far beyond the means at command; so it was decided to retain the main features of their plans modified, however, so as to produce the best possible effects by judiciously arranging and planting trees and shrubs and making the least expensive lakes and water-ways, without the use of statuary, stonework or costly buildings. While public parks are intended to afford the means of pleasant and healthful recreation to all classes and conditions of people, it was considered of the utmost importance that all improvements should be made with the especial view of affording the greatest facilities for their use, by persons who are compelled to spend the whole year in the city, and to whom extensive groves and lawns are of far more value than expensive drives, which cannot be used

CONSERVATORY.

"THE MOUND."

Washington Park.

to any great extent, except by persons of means. The only portion of the park territory that had been made accessible to the public was the northern neck of what was known as the Upper Division, but during 1874 the work was hastened along rapidly, although the Commission found itself hampered in various ways in regard to the financial management of this public enterprise. About 200 acres of the western portion of the park were put under cultivation and then already open air concerts were given weekly in a temporary music pavilion under the direction of Hans Balatka. On these occasions the attendance was so large, that the adjoining grounds had to be thrown open to the public. These open air concerts were as early as 1874 attended by immense crowds of visitors and would have drawn still larger numbers of people, if the fare by street cars from the city would have been reduced from fifteen to five cents—the present charge. During 1874 the third new greenhouse was built and a botanical garden established, which again was abandoned three years later, so as to avoid the large and constantly increasing outlay necessary for its maintenance.

That part of the park, lying between Fifty-sixth and Sixty-seventh streets, Stony Island ave. and Lake Michigan (now Jackson Park and the site of the World's Fair) was originally named Lake Park, the western portion West Park and a tract of twenty acres at the intersection of Western ave. and Pavilion (now Garfield) boulevard, was given the name of Gage Park in memory of George W. Gage, one of the original members of the Commission.

The entire amount of land purchased was 1045 acres and up to 1875 nearly four-fifths of the west division of the park had been improved; the four main boulevards, Grand, Drexel, Garfield and Oakwood were completed and Midway Plaisance had been constructed. The floral department was given in charge of Mr. Fred. Kanst, a gardener of great efficiency and an adept in the art of lawn decoration. During the following years unimproved sections of the territory were brought under cultivation and by December 1, 1880, the Board had acquired title to all the lands required for park purposes and some 200 acres more in the eastern portion. The Commission had to wade through a great deal of annoying litigation, which arose from the various conflicting claims of numerous land owners and agents.

As years rolled by West Park became Washington Park, and Lake Park was named Jackson Park, while the memory of Garfield was honored by changing the name of Pavilion boulevard to Garfield boulevard. In 1884 the construction of a pavement beach and sea wall was commenced in Jackson Park, so as to protect the shore against the inroads of Lake Michigan. It is now finished and forms a fit subject for admiration; it consists of a limestone pavement, which has an average width of forty feet and is composed of blocks averaging twelve inches in depth, laid upon two inches of lake gravel; at the landward edge of the pavement is set a lime-stone curbing and immediately back of this is a concrete flag walk twelve feet in width, for which the "Germania" brand of Portland Cement was used, adjoining a fifty foot drive. The top of the curbing at the back edge of the beach pavement is eight feet seven inches above city datum, being six feet six inches above water level. The surface of the pavement rises from front to rear, not on a regular incline, but in a curved line similar to that formed by the waves upon a sand beach.

The very first attempt at shore protection of a substantial character was made in 1874 at the Fifty-ninth street inlet to Jackson Park and resulted in the building of a north- and south-pier, which has formed the inlet up to the present time. Fitz Simons and Connell constructed about six thousand feet of breakwater, commencing at Fifty-sixth street and running to the present entrance to the World's Fair grounds. This sloping breakwater has proved a great success and, when kept clean of sand and debris, it forms a lovely margin to the blue waters of the lake. Mr. J. Frank Foster, the general superintendent of the South Parks, was the engineer of the work and to him is due largely the credit of having designed so effective and beautiful a shore improvement, as this one has become to be.

In 1876 a part of Washington Park was used as a pasture for a flock of South-down sheep, numbering sixty-eight, but this feature of park-life was soon after discarded.

Quite early in the history of the South Parks the Board entertained the desire to secure control of Michigan ave. and Thirty-fifth street (from Grand boulevard to Michigan avenue), as those streets would form an important link between the City and the Park system. The cost of improving Michigan boulevard so as to harmonize with the character of the other boulevards was estimated at $551,063 and after years of litigation and vexations delay the Commission has at last succeeded in improving the entire length of Michigan ave., from Jackson street to Washington Park, making it one of the finest pleasure drives in the world. About the time parks were decided upon for this city, Dr. G. H. Rauch, for many years the Secretary of the Illinois State Board of Health, in a paper read before the Academy of Sciences of this city, discussed in a very lucid and instructive manner the influence of public parks upon the moral, physical and sanitary condition of the inhabitants of large cities, and although many people may be familiar with the subject in question, it has such an intimate bearing upon the matter presented in this book, that we deem it desirable to republish a short extract therefrom.

After a brief account of the parks in the chief cities of the world, Dr. Rauch goes more fully into the question as it affects the citizens of Chicago and presents many interesting facts regarding its situation and physical relations. Located on the southwest shore of Lake Michigan, the land that stretches back from it is almost as flat and low as the lake itself. The average elevation for five miles around is but twelve feet above the water level, while a large portion of the ground is depressed and swampy, with but little drainage. The land upon which the city stands is the ancient bed of the lake (which has receded far below its former level), and consists of sand-banks, clay-beds, and vegetable mould. From the flatness of the region winds have an unbroken sweep, as there are no mountains, hills, or forests to arrest them. In an area of four hundred square miles surrounding Chicago, there are hardly twenty square miles thinly covered with timber. But, as even the enterprise of Chicago is inadequate to build mountains, and as hills also are very expensive, the city has but one way left to protect itself against its special exposure, and that is, to surround itself with artificial forests.

Another aspect of the subject to which Dr. Rauch draws attention, is the sanitary influence of trees and foliage, the relations of climate to disease and of the parks to mental hygiene, and the special need which so overexcited a people as those of Chicago have for every kind of recreation and diversion. "We need parks to induce out-door exercise, and for the pleasant influences connected with them, which are so beneficial to our over-worked business men, to dyspeptics, to those afflicted with nervous diseases, and, particularly, to the consumptive. We need parks for our school children, as we have no places to which they can resort for out-of-door play, and where they can obtain healthful recreation, with the exception of the limited grounds surrounding the school-houses."

"The moral influence of the parks is decided. Man is brought in contact with Nature—is taken away from the artificial conditions in which he lives in cities; and such associations exercise a vast influence for good."

Dr. Rauch has indeed spoken the truth and the uses of our parks as a means of popular intellectual improvement, and their importance as an educational agency in connection with the great school system of this city, are by no means yet fully recognized. Their rich array of trees, shrubs, and flowers, in their season, are not only objects of attention from their varied beauty, but they minister to a still further and most important use as objects of engaging study to the youth of the schools of Chicago.

The South Parks became more of a resort for the general public after the cable lines in Cottage Grove avenue and State street were completed a few short years ago; previously, on account of the long distance lying be-

Sun Dial in Washington Park.

tween them and the thickly populated districts of the city and the difficulty people, not owners of private conveyances and unable to patronize livery stables, experienced in getting there, these parks principally formed the destination of the upper tendom, the wealthy and fashionable, whose elegant equipages and turnouts thronged the boulevards and park driveways. There the richly attired ladies and stylish looking gentlemen reigned supreme and the common people did not block their way. Thanks to the extension of the afore mentioned cable car-lines way beyond the southern limits of the park territory and to the facilities afforded by the trains of the Illinois Central and the Elevated railway, all leading to these health giving pleasure grounds, men, women and children on foot are now largely in the majority in the South Parks. Especially gratifying is it to witness the signs of joy and happiness, which the little ones seem to feel when brought out here among the green trees and beautiful flowers, where their pale cheeks at once assume a healthier color, their limbs greater elasticity. Even the most distant quarters of the city send large delegations of tenement-house occupants, dwellers in unhealthy, disease-breeding basements to the shady meadows of the South Parks, where they spend many happy hours in the enjoyment of the blessings that kind nature and the handiwork of man have spread out before them in such glorious profusion. As early as 1873 it was found desirable to increase the attractions of Washington Park, by providing a place of resort for children and families who came by cars and were seeking their pleasure within such distances as were easily accessible on foot. To meet this want, a ramble was designed and laid out immediately south of the entrance from Drexel Boulevard and adjacent to the car track on Cottage Grove avenue. The effect of intricacy and variety was secured by means of irregular plantations of shrubbery, to form thickets and copses, interspersed with bits of open ground or broad lawn to serve as play grounds for children. The paths wind about among these scenes, opening new vistas or views at every turn and conveying the impression of a much more extended area than it actually occupies.

We have already endeavored to convey some idea of what the South Parks were, when they were first laid out and came into the hands of the Commissioners, who by the way receive no pay for their services. Since then the improvements have been steadily going forward. Excellent drives, and walks, and bridle paths, and artificial lakes have been constructed and beautiful trees, and shrubs, and evergreens have been judiciously planted to give character and variety to the meadows and lawns; no touch of the landscape gardener could add very considerably to the fresh appearance of its glades and groves, and cool secluded nooks. The public knows how to prize the noble sycamores, the stately maples, the superb catalpas and the large variety of other magnificent trees, that adorn Washington Park and the boulevards. In short, the transformation of these grounds from a sandy waste to beautiful flower-gardens, lawns and shady retreats ever was and still is a great surprise to the public.

In the Park the passing observer is very strongly impressed with the manner in which everchanging views are successively opened before him; views, which possess every quality of complete and impressive landscape compositions. As an authority on landscape gardening remarks: "Other forms of natural scenery stir the observer to warmer admiration, but it is doubtful if any and certain that none which under ordinary circumstances man of set purpose can induce nature to supply him, are equally soothing and refreshing; equally adapted to stimulate simple, natural and wholesome tastes and fancies, and thus to draw the mind from absorption in the interest of an intensely artificial habit of life."

In the improvement of this territory attractive and picturesque scenery has been formed and accommodations were prepared for great numbers of people, each class of which is led to enjoy and benefit by the scenery without preventing or seriously detracting from the enjoyment of it by all others. To repeat, the scenery of Washington Park is diversified and it commands fine distant views. These advantages and its exemption from factory smoke or foul smells compensate for the necessity the citizens are under to travel a number of miles to reach it.

Every thing is useful just in proportion as it in some way adds to human enjoyments and the Park is certainly one of the foremost things, that give pleasure to human beings.

Its civilizing and humanizing influence is something wholly incalculable. The visitors belong to every class and grade of society, and yet every one seems there to be on his good behaviour. The Commissioners have kept steadily in view the one object of making it a pleasure ground; admitting nothing, which would interfere with this, prohibiting nothing which would conduce to it. The regulation formerly quite generally in use in all of our parks: "Keep off the grass," is one of the things of the past in this Park, and any one who has seen the glee with which men, women and children repose or play upon the soft velvet sward, will see how much the actual enjoyment of the Park is enhanced by permitting the free use of the lawns. The toil-worn artisan, his weary wife and pining children are, thanks to the wise fore-thought of the Commissioners, assured that on any bright summer or autumn day they will find sward and shade open to them.

Everything done here is done according to the best rules of the land-scape gardeners art; in the process of grouping as well as in the endeavor to secure those fine contrasts of color which by a proper selection of trees and shrubs, the autumn foliage can be made to display.

According to these rules the Park shows principally the character of free and unrestricted nature, where the hand of man should not be noticed except through well kept walks and drives and the judicious distribution of buildings. The extensive territory Washington and Jackson Park occupy, of which the former contains 371, the latter 586 acres, whereto 100 acres must be added covered by Midway Plaisance, made the construction of park lands possible on a much larger and more imposing scale, than could be done in either of the other four large parks of the city. If it was possible to lift them up and carry them to the South Parks, they would all of them easily find room within the boundaries of Washington and Jackson Park. In the western part of Washington Park, near the entrance from Garfield boule-vard, is situated an open lawn containing one hundred acres, which the Com-missioners have turned over to those fond of playing "lawn tennis," "cricket" and similar out-door sports; the Commissioners even went so far in their praiseworthy anxiety to please the public and make people feel happy, as to purchase the articles necessary for such amusements and to loan them out to the players. This character of open park scenery—of wood without under-growth and of lawn irregularly bounded by groups of large trees—is pre-served in Washington Park throughout in order that it might be left open to the public at all times, by day and by night, without risk of such abuse of its privileges as might exist, if exclusion and concealment were secured by the presence of thickets and copses of shrubbery. The wisdom of such provision for the future, when the neighborhood of the park becomes thickly inhabited, is obvious.

In the immediate vicinity of the aforesaid western park-entrance Mr. Kanst, the head gardener, has obtained very picturesque effects by means of climbing plants, which have crept up over tall tree stumps, from where they droop down in graceful garlands or stretch across shady paths to trees on the other side, thereby forming a canopy of rich foliage.

South of the large baseball lawn lies the glittering park-lake, covering an area of about twenty acres. Its green shore stretches around in graceful curves, where stately trees throw their deep shadows upon the mirror like surface of the water; upon these shores beautiful flowers bloom in great variety and children love to roam and play.

The paths and driveways through the park are without any exception laid out in such a manner, that each one of them will lead the traveler to the most advantageous points of view.

Gates Ajar in Washington Park

Crossing over to the extreme eastern portion of Washington Park we find here the Palm House and just west of it, in the centre of a circuitious driveway, the floral display of Mr. Kanst, his pride and the joy of the public. To get a glimpse of this panorama of flowers and plastic floral designs is indeed worth a journey from a distance. We will not attempt a description of the various figures, emblems, floral fancies as they should be called, carpet-beds rich in colors and unique in design, for everybody interested in flowers and floral decorations, every lover of the sweet-scented children of flora, should personally visit this highly fascinating spot. It required not less than 300,000 plants and flowers to embroider and embellish these emerald lawns, in which number however are included many thousands that were used for beautifying the center of Drexel boulevard and the surroundings of the Drexel fountain at the southern end of said boulevard. A remarkable piece of work and a triumph of art among many floral masterpieces was a portrait of General Grant, which was executed by Mr. Kanst in the spring of 1885 and elicited much favorable and well deserved comment. The interior of the palmhouse with its large variety of tropical and semi-tropical plants will also prove highly interesting to the visitor. Before we take our departure from this beautiful park let us not forget to take a look at the lily-ponds, situated only a few paces south of the palm house, here, among the numerous specimens of the family of water lilies we also behold several fully developed Virginia Regia's, the queenly sea-rose of the tributaries of the Amazon river. It truly deserves to be ranked among the foremost objects of interest and admiration in the floral kingdom, and for those who gather around these ponds with their array of lotus-plants and water-lilies, natives of China, Japan, Africa, Egypt and our own country, it forms the centre of attraction.

We find here Nymphaea odorata, N. alba, N. tuberosa, N. dentata, N. rubra and other species, but, as before remarked, the grandest of them all is the Victoria Regia. Though it was discovered by the botanist Haenke as early as 1801 and scientifically described by Professor Poeppig of Leipzic in 1832, it was not named till 1838, when Lindley dedicated it to his sovereign, and in 1850 it was for the first time introduced into cultivation through the efforts of the traveler Spruce.

The gigantic circular leaves of this wondrous plant measure six feet and more in diameter and have a turned up margin as a border from two to five inches high, giving the leaf the resemblance to a huge tray or salver. The upper surface of this leaf is of a rich green color, while the lower surface shows a purple or violet color and is traversed by ridge-like veins or ribs, which radiate from the centre and are connected by ribs running crossways, so that the entire surface below is divided into air-compartments, which give the leaf great carrying power. By placing a board upon one to distribute the weight, it is capable of holding a child from 10 to 12 years of age. The life of the flower is of short duration, lasting only two days. It opens late in the afternoon and remains open about twelve hours; during that period it is cup-shaped, from 12 to 16 inches across, with hundreds of pure white petals and very fragrant. The second day the flower again opens towards evening, but it now presents an entirely different appearance, for the petals are changed to a rosy pink color, and reflexed in the shape of a coronet, but now odorless. Towards morning the flower again closes, never again to open, and during the day it sadly sinks back into its watery bed, there to ripen its seed.

The maintenance of this grand system of parks: police protection, repairs of roads and footpaths, transplanting of trees, etc., last year required over $200,000, which figures explain better than a detailed description of the work done inside of one year for the good of the public can do, the amount of labor that has been performed.

For those, who are the fortunate owners of a buggy or carriage or who possess the means for hiring one, a drive along the broad and well kept boulevards leading north from Washington Park into the heart of the city, or west, where the boulevard systems of the South Parks and the West Parks join hands, will surely prove a most enjoyable one. Those leading north are Drexel boulevard, Grand boulevard, Oakwood boulevard, Thirty-fifth street boulevard and Michigan boulevard. Drexel boulevard is 200 feet wide; it starts from Washington Park at Fifty-first street near Cottage Grove ave. and terminates at Thirty-ninth street, a point 1½ miles north. It consists of a double roadway, embracing a central ornamental space 100 feet wide, arranged with paths, grass plots, magnificent floral decorations, and planted with trees and shrubs. Elegant and costly residences line this magnificent Boulevard on both sides. During the year 1882 the Drexel Brothers of Philadelphia presented to the Commissioners a costly and superb bronze fountain in memory of their father, after whom also the beautiful Boulevard is named. This fountain is located at the turn of said Boulevard at Fifty-first street and is massive, unique and of beautiful design and workmanship. It is crowned by a life size bronze statue of Drexel. From the northern terminus of this boulevard Oakwood boulevard, a hundred feet wide, extends half a mile west to Grand boulevard, which has a width of 198 feet the entire length from Washington Park (at Fifty-first street) north to Thirty-fifth street, which is exactly two miles. Grand boulevard is on the line with South Park ave., which connects at Fifty-fifth street with Garfield boulevard. It comprises a central drive-way, 55 feet wide, with a grass border 20 feet on each side, planted with rows of trees and separating it from the side roads, which are intended for business traffic. Going north in Grand boulevard we at its northern end enter Thirty-fifth street; for a distance of barely ½ of a mile, from Grand boulevard west to Michigan boulevard, this street is under the control of the Park Board as a necessary link between all the afore mentioned boulevards and Michigan boulevard, which latter leads to the business centre of the city. This boulevard is now finished its entire length, from Fifty-fifth street (Garfield boulevard) to Jackson street, a distance of 5¾ miles, and as a street of palatial residences it has no superior in this or any other country.

A delightful pleasure drive is afforded those, who will select Garfield boulevard (Fifty-fifth street) where it emerges from Washington Park, for a visit to the West Park system. The road here naturally leads us in a westerly direction past fine residences and stores far out into the open country, where dwelling houses as yet are thinly scattered.

Garfield and Western avenue boulevards, the connecting links, have a length of over six miles and the greater part of the way they pass through wide stretches of prairie, which as far as the eye can reach is profusely studded with lovely wild flowers, who merrily bow and nod in the breezes.

That part of the boulevard, which leads from Washington Park directly west over Fifty-fifth street, is called Garfield boulevard in honor of our lamented President, James A. Garfield.

It has a uniform width of 200 feet and is lined on both sides of the main drive way with three rows of shade trees. At the intersection of Western ave., which is distant 3½ miles from the point where Garfield boulevard emerges from Washington Park, the boulevard turns north and follows in the road of Western avenue, from which it has taken its name, for a distance of 2.81 miles, until it reaches the Illinois and Michigan Canal, where it crosses by means of a neat drawbridge, constructed by the South Park Commissioners. Between Fifty-fifth street and this Canal the boulevard is enclosed along the western border for long distances by beautiful shrubs and small groves, that lend an additional charm to the landscape, through which the road passes. We behold here a natural garden, in which we can not fail to see the painstaking care of the gardener with sprinkling cart and pruning knife. North of Thirty-ninth street the boulevard passes through Brighton Park, where a small but very picturesque flower garden enhances the beauty of the immediate vicinity and where stately elms and catalpas throw their cool shade over rustic seats and lovely walks. Western avenue boulevard is 200 feet wide, the same as Garfield boulevard.

Residence of Mrs. Catharine Seipp, Michigan Boulevard and 33d Street.

AREAS AND DISTANCES, S. PARKS AND BOULEVARDS.	Total Area. Acres.	Total Length Miles.	Imp'v'd Drives Miles.
Jackson (East) Park..................................	586	......	1.50
Washington (West) Park.............................	371	......	6.06
Gage Park...	20	......	......
Midway Plaisance..................................	80	......	1.38
Grand boulevard, 198 ft. wide.......................	......	2.00	3.55
Drexel boulevard, 200 ft. wide......................	......	1.48	3.05
Oakwood boulevard, 100 ft. wide....................	......	.50	.50
Michigan avenue boulevard..........................	......	5.73	3.73
Thirty-fifth street boulevard......................	......	.32	.32
Garfield boulevard, 200 ft. wide....................	......	3.50	3.75
Western ave. boulevard, 200 ft. wide................	......	2.81	1.29
Fifty-seventh st. boulevard, 100 ft. wide...........	......	.03	.03
Totals......................................	1057	16.37	25.16

The present **Commissioners** are the following gentlemen: **Joseph Don-nersberger, President; Martin J.** Russell, Auditor; John B. Sherman, **William Best and J. W. Ellsworth. H.** W. Harmon is Secretary and John R. Walsh, Treasurer.

THE WEST CHICAGO PARKS.

The **first** Board of West Chicago Park Commissioners consisted of the following gentlemen: Geo. W. Stanford, President; E. F. Runyan, Auditor; Isaac R. Hitt, Clark Lipe, David Cole, Chas. C. P. Holden and Henry Greenebaum, Treasurer. The act of legislature creating this board was approved Feb. 27, 1869. The commissioners were not appointed by **the** Governor, however, until April 26, nearly two months later. The labor **incident** to selecting the lands necessary for the Parks and public grounds contemplated by the law creating the board, and acquiring the title to the same, **was** greater than was at first anticipated; the conflicting interests of real estate owners and the demands and necessities of the public were to be harmonized. While **the law** prescribed the limits within which these Parks should be located, still **the** particular locality within these limits was a matter left to the discretion and judgment **of** the board.

By a resolution adopted June 25, 1869, the preliminary labor of selecting or designating locations for these public improvements was devolved upon a special committee of three, consisting of Messrs. GREENEBAUM, HITT, and RUNYAN, who spent some time and labor in securing to the public, locations for these Parks which should be accessible to the great mass of the people over some public means of travel, and still be within such distance of the business and residence portion of the city as to be readily accessible to pedestrians and carriages.

Under the law, the board was required **to locate and** establish a Boulevard **running** from the north branch of the Chicago **river**, commencing at a point north **of** Fullerton Avenue, running thence west, **one** mile or more west of Western Avenue, and thence southerly, with such curves and deviations as the board should deem expedient, to the Chicago, Burlington and Quincy railroad line, and **on** line of said Boulevard to establish three Parks: the north Park to be in size not less than 200 acres, to **cost** not to exceed $250,000, to be located north of Kinzie Street; the middle **Park** to be located between Kinzie **and** Harrison Street, **to** be in size **not less than** 100 acres, and to cost not **to exceed** $400,000; the southern Park to be not less than 100 acres in **size, and to** cost not to exceed $250,000, to be located south of Harrison Street, **and north of** the Chicago, Burlington and Quincy railroad **line**,—the aggregate **cost** of Parks and Boulevards not to exceed $1,050,000.

It will be seen that **the** power of the **board was so prescribed** by limitations and restrictions, that the selecting and procuring **of the lands** within the limits designated, and for the price or cost indicated, and **at the same** time within a reasonable distance of the residence portion of the **city, was a** problem of no **easy** solution.

It is only by remembering the sandy **desert** out beyond the former western limits of our city, and the marshy **prairie land of** the years gone by that one can realize the wonders that have **been** worked in making this *seeming* Nature what it is. That thickets and **trees** abound; that vines clamber **up** over trellises and the walls of the great **palm** houses; that calm lakes **reflect** the blue heavens or white clouds; that Nature has been tamed **and** civilized and her ruggedness and her softness woven into a garment for the **earth**—this can only be appreciated **by** remembering how all this territory looked in 1869 or **by seeing how some of the** adjacent similar lots and acres look now. The supply **of this city with** pure lake water **was** the noblest labor, but the gift of its great lungs or breathing places ranks next. They are favorite resorts at all **seasons of the year.** In summer, there **is** the leafy quiet **and** almost breath-

The Humboldt Monument in Humboldt Park.

less stillness of the summer-woods; there is the drowsy hum of the bee, and ceaseless whir-r-r of the humming-bird's wing, as it poises in air before a flower its little body of green and gold. There is the sweet monotony of the splash of fountains or ripple of little cascades, lulling the senses into half-forgetfulness, till one dreams that the noisy city has ceased to exist, and that the enchanted gardens of some new Alhambra environ him forever. There is the deep green of the grass, the darker emerald of the leaves, the density of vines and thickets, the faint perfume of summer flowers; and in the holy hush of imitated Nature the rabbit lifts it great ears and eyes without fear, the splendid peacock suns its great eye-embroidered fan and the stately swans sit motionless on the water, like birds of snow in realms of blue, and await the pleasure of the goddess of the lake.

In autumn, when the spirit of the breeze has invaded the sylvan solitudes, and the genii of the season have fired each thicket with gold and crimson, and strewed the grass with the purpling spoils of all the trees; when the vases overflow with floral treasures and the song-birds wake up to pipe a farewell to the flowers; when the enchanted summer-sleep is broken by the first breath of the spirit of the north and the quick-moving children come to look brighter than the birds and sweeter than the passing flowers—the great Parks are a thing of beauty still.

When winter comes to spread her broad white mantle over the grave of the dead grass and shelter with her cold beauty the delicate roots of the flowers; when the delicate birds and animals (of Lincoln Park) are also sheltered and the lakes harden their bosoms into ice; when beautiful girls and strong men buckle on the steel wings to their feet, and the swiftly-darting forms look like the broken fragments of some rainbow of humanity; when the short winterday has furled itself in the blue blankets of the night and the great moon looks down to flood the white landscape with pale glory and tip every barren branch with silver; or when the modest light of stars hesitates in rivalry with brighter eyes, and electric lights arise and recreate the day—then too, the Parks are beautiful.

On the 15th day of July, 1869, the committee submitted to the public ten plans or suggestions for the locations of the Parks. These were exhibited for ten days thereafter, and offers for the sale of lands and donations of the same invited. The result was that no offers were received, whereupon the committee prepared three other plans or suggestions, which were, on the 5th day of August, submitted to the public, and donations again solicited.

The result was that donation for a portion of the Boulevards were made, and 14 acres promised conditionally, to be used in the purchase of the northern Park. The committee having this matter in charge, made their report to the board on the 19th day of August, setting forth the plans which had been submitted to the public, and reporting the donations made or promised. Final action was not taken on this report until the 4th day of November, 1869, when the board definitely fixed and established the lines and boundaries of Parks and Boulevards.

By the action of the board, a system of public Parks and pleasure ways was secured, which combined all the advantages which the topographical nature of the country afforded, having due regard to the means of access, and proximity to the city. The boundaries of the Parks having been established, the great work undertaken had just been entered upon; to secure the title to these lands at prices which should be fair and equitable, as between the public and the owner, gave rise to prolonged negotiations. The Park Commissioners were in the market desiring to buy these lands, without money or means of getting it until special assessments could be levied and collected. Prices of lands in the vicinity of the Parks, under the excitement which existed during the early part of 1869, had run up to a high figure, from which owners were slow to recede, yet the board was so thoroughly convinced that the prices asked were speculative and not the real value, that they refused to buy except in cases where concessions of from 20 to 25 per cent were made from these extreme prices.

The Commissioners were willing to pay for the lands, taking the value as it should be determined by the assessors appointed by the courts to condemn the same. They were willing to ascertain this value without appealing to the court, and much time and labor was expended in establishing or agreeing upon the true rule to be followed in determining this question. That insisted upon by the board, was to enquire what was the value of the lands taken for the improvement contemplated at the time the same were selected, without regard to any effect which the contemplated improvements might have upon other lands in the vicinity.

Upon this basis, substantially, the purchases were conducted—making the purchase money payable in three installments, thus dividing the special assessments into three annual assessments, instead of raising it by one assessment, as would have been necessary if the land had been secured by condemnation.

The resources of the board from which to realize money to pay for lands thus purchased, were. 1. The power to levy and collect special assessments upon the real estate deemed benefited. 2. The right to issue bonds to pay the amount found payable by the public; and 3. To issue bonds to pay any deficiency which might exist after exhausting the other resources of the board.

The first assessment made by the assessors was for the sum of $231,835.73, which was confirmed by the Circuit Court, and extended on the general Tax Warrant for the year 1870. The amount collected under this warrant, less commission for collecting, was $169,887.51, the balance, $55,810.91, was reported to the County Court at the August term, 1871, as delinquent, and judgment rendered against the property. Parties contesting this tax in the County Court perfected appeals from this judgment to the Circuit Court about the 15th day of September following, and were pending in the Circuit Court at the time of the destruction of the records of said Court by the great fire, October 9, 1871. Accordingly, measures were taken to restore the Record of Appeals taken by delinquent owners; and the second assessment authorized by law, amounting to $212,108.51, was made, and reported to the Circuit Court for confirmation.

During the year 1871, four artesian wells were sunk, one in each of the parks, and one in Humboldt Boulevard. The sinking of these wells was then a matter of necessity, as at that time the municipal water mains did not extend to those distant parts of the city. The well in Central Park is 1,220 feet deep, the one in Douglas Park 1,165 and the well in Humboldt Park 1,155 feet deep. The well in Humboldt Boulevard is located in Maplewood, at a point nearly midway between the eastern terminus of the Boulevard and Logan Square.

In 1868, the year before the Park Act was passed, the land added by this Act to the city, were assessed and paid taxes on a valuation of $429,660; in 1872, the same lands were assessed and paid taxes on a city assessment of $9,596,230. This increase in the value of real estate was attained during a period of the time most trying to the City of Chicago and its interests—a fearful conflagration in a few hours wiping out of existence a vast amount of its wealth, utterly ruining many of its most active citizens, and followed in a few months by a depression in business generally, reaching to every person in the country, with a stringency in money centres which for a time threatened the overthrow of all classes; yet through it all, these lands have steadily from year to year advanced, and they have been an important element in securing this result, *without* which other important interests would have been diverted to more favorable localities; they have formed the nucleus around which all other interests have centered.

Soon after the terrible conflagration of Oct. 8 and 9, 1871, it was suggested by the city press that, with relics from the ruins, a monument ought to be erected in Garfield Park, which should be unique in construction, and serve to commemorate in some degree the fearful effect of the fiery elements which had swept over the fairest portion of our city. Seizing upon the suggestion thus made, the Board adopted a plan, affording opportunity to cut in lasting marble the grateful acknowledgments of a suffering city. The ceremony of laying the corner-stone came off on the 30th of October, 1872, when it was laid with Masonic ceremonies, in the presence of a large number of citizens. From the address of Hon. S. S. Hayes, who was one of the principal speakers on that occasion, the following may be quoted in reference to the great Chicago fire:

Residence of Wm. Schmidt, near Lincoln Park.

"On the night of Oct. 8th, 1871, the Great Fire broke forth and raged with resistless fury until the close of the next day, when by the blessing of Divine Providence its ravages were stayed.

It was the greatest conflagration of which history gives an account, unless we except the burning of Moscow on the 15th and 16th of September, 1812. The great fire in London in 1666 did not equal it in extent, or the amount of loss. The London fire swept a space a mile long and half a mile wide, and the value of buildings and goods consumed was estimated at from fifty to sixty million dollars. In the burning of Moscow, the private loss by the destruction of houses and their contents, exclusive of public buildings, was calculated at one hundred and fifty millions of dollars. The Chicago fire devastated a space nearly a mile in width and three miles and a half in length, containing two thousand acres. Forty churches, fifty hotels, and nearly all the public buildings, newspaper offices, banks, theatres and finest wholesale and retail storehouses, besides thousands of dwellings, many of the most costly character, were laid in ashes. The number of buildings destroyed was 17,450; of persons rendered homeless, 98,500. The losses on property of all descriptions aside from depreciation of land, were estimated at two hundred millions of dollars. No one who beheld those terrible scenes can ever forget them. The earth and air for miles a pandemonium of flames, full of all horrors, the roaring hurricane of fire sweeping down and devouring massive blocks of brick, stone and iron as though they were wood, terror-stricken people half clad crowding the streets and fleeing for their lives, some into the water of Lake Michigan, others to the suburbs and adjacent country, over one hundred thousand men, women and children without shelter or food, the water supply destroyed, the firemen and police worn out or saving their families, no hope of preserving any part of the city except from the continuance of the south-west wind—such was the dreadful scene that neither tongue nor pen can describe. And through these trying scenes what self-sacrifice, what devotion, what tenderness, what endurance, feeble women carrying from the flames the aged and infirm, little children suppressing their terror to comfort their stricken parents, and men became giants in energy, and everywhere risking their lives, and spending their last strength to rescue the helpless, and save them from impending death.

A few brave men were still fighting the fire, and mining the buildings with gunpowder, on the South Side, others trying to rescue and succor the helpless. A little band of heroes from Milwaukee were making the last stand with their engines at Indiana street bridge. The last almost hopeless efforts were blessed with success. The fire was arrested and driven slowly from its prey. But the great and beautiful city was in ashes; its glory and its pride were in the dust, a boundless expanse of blackened ruins. For miles there was no sight or sound of life, only smoking heaps, solitary chimneys and towers, broken portals and ragged and tottering walls, with here and there the spectral outline of some great building empty and roofless and bare, a mournful scene of lonely desolation. We all know that Chicago has risen again in greater magnificence than before. This was to be expected from the speedy resurrection of Rome, of London and of Moscow. It was also to be expected from the sagacity, the foresight, the patient industry, the indomitable courage and the high intelligence of our people. Individuals have lost their all, but the city knows no loss; it stands with its resources undiminished, its trade, its population, the value of its property largely increased. The burnt district in the business quarter in a single year has been mostly rebuilt in a style of greater solidity and of surpassing beauty. Two-thirds of the dwellings have been restored. In another year scarcely a vestige of the Great Fire will remain. This monument is being erected to keep that event in remembrance, to make known to future ages our sense of its magnitude, our thankfulness to a merciful Providence for our rapid recovery, and our heart-felt and endless gratitude to a sympathising world for their over-flowing kindness, their unmeasured benefactions in the time of our suffering."

Central Park was opened to the public in August, 1874, and the throng of people who visited the park on the occasion, and the concert days thereafter, was a highly satisfactory demonstration of the interest taken in the parks.

From the origin of the West Park Board in 1869, until March 1st, 1877, the important offices and practical control of the Board had been in the same hands, until the retirement of E. F. Runyan, in the fall of 1876 and the appointment of Hon. J. F. A. **Muus** as his successor caused a change in the balance of power, resulting in the election of Clark Lipe, President; Alden C. Millard, Secretary, and B. **Loewenthal, Esq.**, President of the International Bank, Treasurer; instead of Messrs. Stanford President, and Greenebaum Treasurer, who had from the first occupied their respective positions.

The Governor, at this time, attempted to remove four of the members, namely: Clark Lipe, **President; A. C. Millard**, Secretary; **A.** Muus and **C. C. P** Holden, from the office of Park Commissioners; and on October 8th, 1877, each of the Commissioners named received a communication from the Governor, from which the following is an extract:

SIR: It has been evident for some time that the Board of West Chicago Park Commissioners, as at **present** constituted, has lacked the harmony necessary to enable it to do its duty in a manner which should be a credit to the individual members, and command the respect and confidence of the citizens of the town of West Chicago. The Board is divided into two parties, which seem to be irreconcilable, each demanding the removal of the whole or part of the opposing faction. I am fully convinced that in their capacity of Commissioners, the present members of the Board of West Chicago Park Commissioners do not possess the kind of qualifications which are necessary to the discharge of the duties of said office, and that the successful administration of the Parks of West Chicago demands a change in said Board. I, therefore, by virtue of the power vested in me by the Constitution of the State of Illinois, do hereby remove C. C. P. Holden, Alden C. Millard, Clark Lipe, and J. F. **Adolph Muus**, West Chicago Park Commissioners, and declare their offices vacant.
S. M. CULLOM,
Governor

On October 11th the Governor appointed the following named gentlemen West Chicago Park **Commissioners:** Peter Schüttler to succeed C. C. P Holden, Emil Wilken to **succeed** Alden C. Millard, Sextus N. Wilcox to succeed Clark Lipe, and E. **E. Wood** to succeed J. F. Adolph Muus. Peter Schüttler declined to accept the said appointment as to himself, and thereupon the Governor appointed John Brenock in his place.

The Commissioners removed pronounced the Governor's action illegal and unconstitutional and appealed to the courts for protection. Long and weary litigation followed, and by a decision of the Supreme Court the Governor was sustained in his removals; the assumption of a life interest in the office of Commissioner was limited to a term of seven years.

The new administration, although organized on the 15th of March, 1878, did not gain possession of the office, books and documents until the 5th day of July following, when the financial affairs of the Board were found to be in an unsatisfactory condition; some time was required to ascertain the amount of the immediate liabilities of the Board for men's wages, bills for supplies for the Parks and amount of overdue interest, and the available resources to meet such claims.

The new Board of Commissioners was composed of the following gentlemen. Willard Woodard, President; Samuel H. McCrea, Sextus N. Wilcox, John Brenock, Auditor; Emil Wilken, E. Erwin Wood, George Rahlfs, Berthold Loewenthal was Treasurer and R. McChesney Secretary. The following year Mr. John Buehler was appointed Treasurer and E. E. Wood Secretary.

Many of the primary plans for developing the grounds and obtaining the best results from the unpromising blank on which first to operate—a flat, naked, cold and undrained prairie of clay, destitute of any natural beauty, in landscape or otherwise—were of necessity experimental, and in some instances required the handling and re-handling of earth two or three times to obtain satisfactory results. Earth suited to the requirements of tree, shrub and lawn nature had not supplied, and without a soil loamy and rich, no shady grove or velvety lawn was possible. To supply this necessity, therefore, it became necessary to make up artificially large quantities of compost, involving much

HUMBOLDT PARK

HUMBOLDT PARK, CHICAGO.

labor and expense in collection and subsequent treatment of its ingredients. Garfield (then Central) Park was the first battle ground. The experimental park, though only partially developed, was thrown open to public use fully four years before either of the others, and during these four years the Park management were gaining in experience and wisdom, which accrued to the benefit of the other parks when active work was commenced therein. This work was continued in Douglas and Humboldt Parks under more favorable conditions. Labor and material were cheaper, and with the experience obtained a given sum of money obtained a greater and more perceptible amount of improvement than a like sum would or could have done during the earlier labors of the Board. And, fortunately for the taxpayers, arrangements were concluded by the Board by which two of the largest railway companies entering Chicago disposed of the earth and ordure from their stock cars so that it was conveniently situated and readily available for use in any of the parks. The debit value of Garfield Park was increased by an abortive attempt to commemorate the great fire of 1871 by the afore mentioned monument, which entailed a cost of nearly $14,000, and which has long become a part of the earth surrounding it.

Up to 1882 the citizens could not expect rapid development, much less great perfection of Park and Boulevards, while the Board had but the limited revenue of $100,000 from which all expense, both of new work and maintaining the old was taken. Thereafter a petition was presented and a bill introduced to the Legislature, providing for an additional tax of two and one-half mills, which added nearly $90,000.00 to the income.

A movement sprung up in 1880 among certain property owners on the line of Humboldt Boulevard, with the intention to secure the building of a driveway similar to that connecting Garfield and Humboldt Parks, to extend north and east, and eventually connect with some similar driveway extending west from Lincoln Park. The Board then owned in the town of Jefferson the right of way for Boulevard purposes, extending north and east from Humboldt Park to Western Avenue, a distance of about 13,000 feet. That town at that time contributed in part the expense of grading and of planting trees.

As a whole, there was probably never on this continent, nor in the old world, such a grand and complete conception of pleasure grounds and drives as was here presented. A great commercial mart of then over half a million souls, with rapidly increasing wealth and population, with untiring energy, and every condition that was necessary to insure its future position as the great metropolis of this continent, encircled on every side by park and driveway, so developed, improved and perfected as shall render it a garden indeed; a restful spot, a breathing space of pure air, and free as the drawn breath to the thousands who may seek its quiet and repose; open to the son of toil and capitalist alike, and of such ample space as will meet the demands of a city of millions; surely the apprehension of this great idea was worthy of the far-sighted appreciation of the intelligent citizens of Chicago, and of the coming wants of this great city when its ample wealth shall insist upon the development of the esthetic as well as the material growth of its inhabitants.

With such encouragement and material aid as was afforded by the intelligence and wealth which made up the city's greatness, one could with reason expect that the present generation would be able to enjoy the pleasure of twenty-five miles of continuous driving, commencing at Lincoln Park on the north (a wonder in itself) then west, south and east through woodland and grove, by gravel road and rustic viaduct, by lake and stream and bubbling fountain, by greensward and velvety lawn, the air redolent with the perfume of a thousand flowers, and song of bird as clear and free as in virgin forest; till South Park, with all its grand appointments, is reached on the south.

· In 1881 the Board of West Chicago Park Commissioners consisted of the following gentlemen: Harvey L. Thompson, Consider B. Carter, George Rahlfs, Samuel H. McCrea, John Brenock, Willard Woodard, Sextus N. Wilcox, and J. Frank Lawrence. S. H. McCrea was President; John Buehler, Treasurer; Willard Woodard, Auditor; Thomas J. Suddard, Secretary, and O. F. Dubuis, Engineer. Mr. Wilcox was drowned in Lake Superior in June,

1881, and Mr. J. Frank Lawrence appointed to succeed him. John Brenock, who was elected President of the Board in 1882, resigned that office in March of that year, and Patrick J. McGrath succeeded him.

In connection with Mr. Wilcox, it may be mentioned, that early in the spring of 1878, he attempted to remove the treasurer of the board, Mr. Berthold Löwenthal, from office and for no other perceptible reason than that Mr. Löwenthal refused to make loans out of the funds of his bank to the board, who at that time had to battle with might and main against financial difficulties. The demand for his resignation was sent to him in writing, but the sender had chosen a very inappropriate time for the delivery of the message, for on that very day Mr Löwenthal was carrying to the grave two of his beloved children, who had suddenly been torn from him by relentless death. As no charges could be brought against Mr. Löwenthal, he of course paid no heed to the ill-timed peremptory demand, and remained in office to the end of his term.

In accordance with an act of the State Legislature, and a petition signed by the owners of a majority of the frontage of the abutting property, the City Council, on September 29, 1879, conveyed by ordinance to the Board of Commissioners the control of Washington Street, from Halsted Street to Garfield Park. On October 17, 1879, the Board, by formal action, secured control, and in 1881 the work was put under contract from Halsted Street to Rockwell Street.

The Board of West Chicago Park Commissioners, in the years 1883-4, was constituted as follows: Henry S. Burkhardt, Patrick McGrath, Harvey L. Thompson, Christian C. Kohlsaat, George Rahlfs, David W. Clark and John Brenock, and in 1885-6 the members of the Board were the following: Christoph Tegtmeyer, Henry S. Burkhardt, Patrick McGrath, Harvey L. Thompson, Christian C. Kohlsaat, George Rahlfs, David W. Clark, with George Rahlfs as President.

In the year 1885 contracts were let for the new greenhouse in Garfield Park and for the new conservatory in Humboldt Park. The green-houses are composed of stone foundations, brick substructures and wood, and consist of exotic houses, hot, cold and propagating houses, boiler, fuel, potting and store rooms, offices, passages and entrance porches. The Humboldt Park houses were built with glass superstructures, and cover an area of about 15,000 square feet, divided as follows: Exotic house, 48x64 feet and 62 feet high; hot and cold houses 25x60 feet each, and four propagating houses, each 12x100 feet, and the remainder of the buildings for working rooms and passages. This plant is so arranged that the large and lofty exotic house is in the centre, surmounted by two cupolas, with hot and cold houses as wings at the sides, entrance porches and offices in front, and working rooms in the rear, the propagating houses radiating from the same. The Garfield Park plant covers an area about as great as that at Humboldt, divided as follows: An exotic house 48x48 feet, and 63 feet high, hot and cold houses 26x55 feet each, and four propagating houses 12x100 feet each, and the remainder for working rooms and passages. The Garfield plant is so arranged that the exotic house, octagonal in shape and surmounted by a dome and cupola, occupies the center, with hot and cold houses as wings on either side, entrance porches and offices in front and working rooms in the rear, the propagating houses radiating from the same. Each plant is heated by a hot water system skilfully constructed, and so arranged that each house is independent of the other, and the water, after passing through about 7,000 feet of pipe, returns to the two large boilers to be re-heated. The main houses are covered with ribbed glass, decorated with stained glass, and have cement walks. The Humboldt Park conservatory was built at a cost of $22,594.08, and that in Garfield Park at about the same amount.

Union Park, located just east of Ashland Avenue, on the line of Washington Boulevard, was, by ordinance of the City Council passed October 9, 1885, turned over to the Board of West Chicago Park Commissioners, and the Board accepted the control of same by ordinance passed October 12, 1885. This Park, with Washington Boulevard extended through it, provided quite an acquisition to the Park system. It was acquired by the city by purchase from S. S. Hayes, W. S. Johnston, Samuel L. Baker and others, in December, 1853, and February, 1854. It contains 14 4·5 acres and is bounded by West Lake Street, Bryan Place, Ogden, Warren and Ashland Avenues.

Union Park was improved a few years ago as follows: The lake is divided into three parts: First, one basin 300x200 feet, of an oval form; the contours are regular and defined by a moulded stone coping laid on stone foundations. Opposite Park Avenue is a lake landing 66 feet long and 35 feet wide, divided in its center by broad stone steps, and ornamented with stone pedestals for vases and flagstaff. The central feature is a canal 30 feet wide and 75 feet long, spanned by a stone bridge. The third feature is a basin 100 feet in diameter, with stone railing and central decorative fountain. These basins are of Portland cement concrete, and the water in each is six inches on the edges, gradually deepening to three feet in the center. The walks are well shaded, furnished with seats, and are much easier of ingress and egress than formerly.

The office building erected in Union Park during 1888 at a cost of $15,864.60 is a picturesque structure, set back from frequented paths, as befits its purely business and private character, and forms an agreeable feature of the park landscape. It has a stone basement, with a brick and frame super-structure and a one-story roof of the English cottage style, the gables being built with exterior timber and sluice panels. The entrance is through a veranda under the roof to the main business office, handsomely partitioned off, with a meeting room for the Board and offices for the President, Secretary and General Superintendent. In the basement are toilet rooms for ladies and gentlemen and a storage room for tools and implements. The interior finish of the building is of red oak, and the walls are sand finished and painted a neutral green. Three large vaults have been built to accommodate the large mass of books and papers which have accumulated. The conservatory is limited in extent, its contents consisting principally of palms and ferns, but nevertheless a very pretty view as seen from the Board room windows. A graceful winding staircase leads up the interior of the tower, and to the rooms for the janitor and gardener. The material excavated from the basement has been utilized in filling the surroundings of the building and forming new lawns and terraces. A new driveway with an entrance from Bryan Place has also been constructed. The total cost of the improvements has been $19,135.09.

Vernon Park, located on the line of Polk Street, between Center Avenue and Loomis Street, was on October 12, 1885, turned over to the Board of West Chicago Park Commissioners, who accepted control of same by ordinance passed November 9, 1885. This park, covering an area of four acres, laid about four feet below the level or grade of the surrounding property. Thirteen thousand four hundred and sixty-three dollars and sixty-five cents were expended in re-constructing this park. The total park area has been raised above the street grade, over 25,000 cubic yards of clay, sand and black soil have been used in the filling, 382 trees have been planted and 603 feet of stone curbing set. The park now is one of the most beautiful of the small parks in the city. It is in the center of a large and rapidly improving district, and will perhaps confer as much real benefit and pleasure to the public as any improvement heretofore made in our parks. It was donated to the city by Henry D. Gilpin, October 17, 1859, and is bounded by Macalister and Gilpin Places, Loomis, Sibley and Lytle Streets and Centre Avenue.

Jefferson Park, located between Monroe and Adams Streets on the north and south and Throop and Loomis on the east and west, is a pretty little park of about five and one-half acres. It is in the form of a square, and is surrounded on all sides by fine residences. This park was, by ordinance of the City Council passed October 9, 1885, turned over to the Board of West Chicago Park Commissioners.

Wicker Park, triangular in shape, located between Robey, Park and Fowler streets, in the northwest portion of the city, was turned over to the West Chicago Park Commissioners October 26, 1885. This park is inclosed on all sides by handsome residences, mostly owned by well-known and well-to-do Germans and Scandinavians.

The public spirit of the people of West Chicago took form during the early winter of 1891 and resulted in the passage by the General Assembly of this State of an Act, approved by Governor Joseph W. Fifer on the 12th day of June, 1891, authorizing the corporate authorities of the town of West Chicago to issue bonds for the purpose of improving and completing the parks and boulevards held, controlled and maintained by the Board of West Chicago Park Commissioners, excepting therefrom, however, all boulevards acquired from pre-existing streets. In compliance with the provisions of this Act, such proper action was taken on June 30, 1891, by the corporate authorities of the town of West Chicago, as was necessary to place in the hands of the Park Board bonds of the town of West Chicago aggregating the total sum of one million dollars, to be applied in improvements of the original Park and Boulevard system as specified in such Act of the General Assembly. These bonds are payable within a period of twenty years from the first day of July, 1891, with semi-annual interest thereon at the rate of five per cent. per annum. In order to secure the payment of the interest on those bonds as it becomes due from time to time, and also to pay and discharge the principal thereof, according to the provisions of said Act, as the same shall mature, the corporate authorities of the town of West Chicago, in strict compliance with their legal duties under the constitution and laws of the State of Illinois, have provided for the levy and collection of an annual tax of one and one-half mills of the dollar on all of the taxable property of the town of West Chicago. The bonds so issued and delivered by the town authorities of the town of West Chicago to the West Chicago Park Commissioners are of the denomination of one thousand dollars each. The amount received by the Park Board applicable to general park purposes during the year 1891 was but one hundred and ninety-four thousand six hundred and twenty-six dollars and eighty-three cents. Of this amount one hundred and fifty-seven thousand eight hundred and thirty-four dollars and fifty-one cents were expended in the maintenance of the park system as it was then, leaving the sum of thirty-six thousand seven hundred and ninety-two dollars, thirty-two cents for expenditure upon new improvements. The extension of improvements upon the park system necessarily increased the amount necessary for the purpose of maintenance, and without the timely provision of the one million dollars obtained through the legislation above referred to, it would have been many years before the system of parks could have been completed. The burden to the tax-payer occasioned by the issue of the one million dollar bonds is imperceptible when the beneficent results of a complete park system are considered and appreciated. These bonds came to the aid of the West Chicago Park Commissioners in a most opportune time, and enabled the Board to place its parks and pleasure-ways in a most attractive condition at all times, and especially for the delight and enjoyment of the millions who are our guests during the World's Columbian Exposition. Contracts were at once awarded for all the material necessary in the construction of the boulevards and for the completion of the unimproved portions of Douglas, Garfield and Humboldt Parks, and for such additional buildings as have been deemed necessary

Contracts were also let for the construction of a bridge across the west branch of the south branch of the Chicago river and the building of a bridge in conjunction with the South Park Commissioners across the Illinois and Michigan Canal; both bridges were built within the South-West Boulevard. The construction of these two bridges effectually unites the South Park and the West Park systems, and gives to the world a public pleasure-way unsurpassed anywhere in length, width and attractiveness for pleasure seekers.

On March 14th, of this year, Governor Altgeld appointed the following as members of the West Chicago Park Board:

John W. Garvey to suceed George Mason, Edmund Z. Bradowski to succeed John Kralovec, resigned; Andrew J. Graham to succeed Hermann Weinhardt, resigned; Carl Moll to succeed Harvey L. Thompson resigned; and James J. Townsend to succeed Jefferson L. Fulton, resigned.

Scene in Humboldt Park.

HUMBOLDT PARK.

This popular pleasure garden is situated in the northwestern part of the city, the two main entrances being on California Avenue at the intersection of this street with Division Street and North Avenue. It offers to friends of nature a greater wealth of picturesque views and sylvan retreats, than any other of our artificial forests and is especially fortunate in having been laid out and fostered by enlightened taste and skill, displayed in a high degree by Mr. Frederick Karnatz, the veteran landscape gardener and superintendent of this charming park. Here as in all of our other large public parks much money was spent in ornamental and landscape gardening, the fruits of which, the large number of noble trees, judiciously and picturesquely planted, add the greatest value to these grounds. Of course here too all the landscape, so to speak, had to be manufactured, but the grounds being naturally somewhat higher than those at Garfield and Douglas Parks, less difficulty was encountered in preparing the waste lands for their blessed purpose. The main feature of Humboldt Park is to be found in the magnificence and healthy appearance of the great number and large variety of shade trees. The well kept driveways and footpaths leading through the length and width of the park present a series of natural vistas of land and lake scenery, which break like sudden glimpses of fairy-land upon the gaze of the delighted pilgrim from the hot and dusty city. A net-work of such drives and walks leads deftly over hilly formations, through forest-like groves, through glade and glen; they take us from changing sunshine to shadow, from the margin of the glittering lake to beds of fragrant flowers, to ever recurring vistas of rare beauty and variety — these, and the skilful arrangement of the flower garden in front of the palm house, the judicious grouping of blooming shrubberies here and there and many other beautiful things besides have transformed this spot into one of the loveliest and most delightful suburban parks in this country.

It was opened to the public in July 1877, but was at that time only partially completed. The Germans of Chicago, of whom a large number reside in the northwestern part of the city and the vicinity of the park, were greatly pleased when this park was named after the great naturalist and master in science, Alexander von Humboldt, their illustrious countryman, and they celebrated the day of the opening, it being a Sunday, in regular German fashion. They had a large and imposing street-procession, which was followed at the park by music, song and speeches, the whole taking the shape of a highly enjoyable "Volksfest."

The promise given by Humboldt Park at that early day, when it yet was in its infancy, has been faithfully kept, thanks to the skilful hand of the aforementioned landscape gardener. In no other of our parks is the separation of the system of park-landscapes from that of garden-landscapes so plainly visible and so ably carried through as in this model-park. Humboldt Park has an area of 200 acres, of which in 1891 only half were under cultivation. Since then however the entire northwestern part which until then had been a barren waste, has been taken in hand by a host of workmen, who are transforming all that territory into beautiful groves, lawns, drives and lakes. For these extensive improvements the board of commissioners appropriated no less than $220,000, this sum being a part of the $1,000,000 derived from the sale of bonds authorized by the state legislature. The new work comprises the excavations for a new lake, which will have an average width of 400 feet and will cover an area of about 31 acres. On its northern shore a handsome Casino, to cost $60,000, is now in the course of construction; it will be three stories high, and beneath it on the lakeshore will be the boat landing-place. This part of the park was also chosen for the erection of a handsome music-pavilion and promises as a whole to add quite an attractive feature to lovely

Humboldt Park. All these improvements were greatly hindered in their progress by the long weeks of rainy weather in the spring of 1892, to which is owing the fact, that instead of bringing this new section to completion at the end of last year, it will not be ready for public use before next fall.

On the 16th day of October last (1892) there was unveiled in this park a very handsome bronze statue of Alexander von Humboldt, after whom the park was named. Fully 20,000 persons—some enthusiasts go so far as to claim double that number— witnessed the dedication. Even the lesser number was a tremendous outpouring considering the limited means of transportation to the beautiful park. The occasion was one long to be remembered, not only by the thousands of Germans who participated, but by the countless numbers of other nationalities present. Vast as was the crowd, it testified in mute though powerful manner to the truism that a truly great man belongs to no one nation. It seemed as if by silent agreement all the speakers on this occasion had taken this truism as their leading thought, for all dwelt upon the fact that, abstruse as scientific research of necessity is, Humboldt had in a rare degree the faculty of teaching all people of whatever nation and whatever walk in life. It was a glorious and impressive tribute to the great man's "Kosmos." There was, of course, a grand parade of civic societies; there was "music by the band" as well as by vocal societies, and there was an elaborate oratorical programme—separately and together effective, but far more impressive than it all was the great throng of people that was massed around the central space in front of the old pavilion, where the bronze figure of Humboldt stands, the earnest face whith its massive brow and the sharply accentuated features turned toward the rising sun. The Humboldt statue, the generous gift of Mr. F. J. Dewes, a prominent and highly respected German citizen of Chicago, is pronounced by connoisseurs a masterpiece of the sculptor's art. It was cast in the famous foundry of Gladenbeck & Son, in the German capital. Its height is ten feet and it shows the great savant in the position of a lecturer. In the half raised right hand, which rests against the body, he holds a flower, while the left, in which is clasped a book, rests easily upon the limb of the tree trunk by his side. Partly visible is a globe at his feet, alongside of which the head of an animal and other symbolic figures are seen, indicating the various sciences in which the great naturalist excelled. The whole breathes truth and warmth, pulsating life; the figure shows noble dignity, and the artist has admirably succeeded in portraying Humboldt's nobility of soul, genius and self-reliance. The observer is deeply impressed with the repose and equipoise so dominant in this work of art, and by all real artists considered the first law of sculpture. The monument is an original work of Felix Goerling, a young German artist of rare talents. The granite pedestal was designed and executed by H. C. Hoffman & Co., of this city. It is made from the celebrated Freeport, Me., granite. The ceremony of unveiling the statue was conducted under the auspices of the German Press club. The first step in the direction of making arrangements worthy of the occasion was taken by several friends of F. J. Dewes, the donor of the statue, during his absence in Europe last summer. A committee of thirteen was chosen, and as a large majority of these were also associate members of the German Press club, the desire was expressed that this organization should take full charge of the preparations. The entire committee, to which two members of the Humboldt Celebration club—an organization formed for the sole purpose of arranging the parade of societies who participated in the ceremonies—were added, was as follows:

A. C. Hesing,	Ed. Uihlein,	John Buehler,
C. H. Plautz,	Louis Wolff,	J. Rosenthal,
Harry Rubens,	Edward Rose,	H. Greenebaum,
J. Goldzier,	A. St. George,	Dr. H. Harms,
H. Weinhardt,	F. Amberg,	Edward Koch,
Andreas Simon,	Theo. Janssen,	Dr M. Henius,
Paul Haedicke,	F. Glogauer,	J. P. Arnold,
Dr. F. H. Bernard,	E. F. L. Gauss,	Felix L. Senff.
Carl Haerting,		

Henry Greenebaum was selected as chief marshal and Jacob Gross, George Heinzmann and Franz Amberg were his aids. The arrangements in the park, for seating the distinguished guests, several hundred singers, and particularly for handling the vast crowds were in charge of Park Commissioner Weinhardt, and it is but just to state that not a single hitch occurred to mar the impressiveness of the scene. The formal programme opened with the arrival of the parading societies, twenty in number and several thousand strong, held well in line by Major Heinzmann, the chief of staff. The Humboldt Select Knights of America, in very handsome regalia, formed a circle around the veiled statue and Professor Haud's orchestra intoned a hymnus, which was followed by Mohr's Cantata. "At the Altar of Truth," executed by the following singing societies, under direction of Gustav Ehrhorn: Teutonia Maennerchor, Schiller Liedertafel, Liedertafel Vorwaerts, Freie Saengerbund, Humboldt Saengerclub, Almira Saengerclub. Then Mr. A. C. Hesing, president of the monument committee, formally presented the statue to the west park board in a German speech full of his characteristic vigor and earnestness. Formal though the remarks of necessity were, Mr. Hesing was again and again interrupted by applause, especially when in conclusion he said: "This monument will not only be an ornament to the city, but it will prove a mighty incentive to deep thought and intellectual activity to every beholder. Douglas, Drexel, Martin Ryerson's Indian group, Schiller, Lincoln, LaSalle, Linnæus and Grant ornament our parks and give silent but effective proof of the drift of our people. For Alexander von Humboldt no better place could have been chosen than this beautiful park that bears his name."

Then, amid the vociferous cheers of the thousands, little Martha Weinhardt, daughter of the park commissioner, unveiled the statue, and when Chief Marshal Greenebaum deposited two beautiful floral tributes from the Schlaraffia and from the Citizens' club of Avondale upon the pedestal, cheers upon cheers were given by the multitude.

Harvey L. Thompson, president of the West park board, accepted the magnificent gift in a speech full of enthusiasm, in which he said: To the people of Chicago the present occasion is one for sincere congratulation. The thoughtful and generous gift of Mr. Dewes to the people of this city is another evidence of that large hearted interest manifested by so many public spirited gentlemen by contributing in a public way something to the adornment of our public places and pleasure grounds. Chicago is without a rival in the extent and magnificence of her pleasure domains and the splendid work of art presented to us to-day by one of our citizens and neighbors is an assured promise that the high born spirit of her people, destined to make Chicago peerless among the cities, will also secure to her public places those works of art—those fascinating expressions of the human affections, which so aptly illustrate the progress of an intrepid and exalted civilization.

Mayor Washburne made a happy speech on behalf of the city and Dr. Max Henius, president of the German Press club, paid a masterly tribute to Humboldt in a speech in the German language. The English oration of the occasion was by Professor Albion W Small, of the University of Chicago. He expressed his sincere regret that Professor von Holst, who at first had been invited, had not yet sufficiently recovered his strength to be present. However, the desire to offer a courtesy to the University of Chicago by giving a part in the celebration to some one of its members, was a mark of distinction which it was an honor to acknowledge.

Another monument will soon adorn this park. It will be a statue of Fritz Reuter, the Charles Dickens of the "Plattdeutsche" people. The money has all been subscribed and the statue is to be cast in one of the celebrated foundries of Germany.

GARFIELD PARK.

Not until after the death of President Garfield, was the name of Central Park changed to Garfield Park and then the change was made as a tribute to the memory of the illustrious dead.

This Park is situated about midway between Humboldt and Douglas Parks, about four to five miles from the Court House. It is reached by the Madison Street, Lake Street and Randolph Street car lines and by Washington Boulevard The Central Boulevard from Humboldt to Garfield Park has been handsomely improved during the last season and now furnishes to owners of private vehicles an elegant roadway for a pleasure drive. A very important improvement on the line of this boulevard is the viaduct over the Chicago, Milwaukee and St. Paul Railway tracks, the roadway of which has been paved by the Railroad Company, who also erected a substantial railing on each side of it. This viaduct was thrown open for public travel May 15, 1886. Considerable planting was done on the approaches leading to this structure and nearly all the ornamentation with shrubs and trees was executed under the personal supervision of Mr. George Rahlfs, then commissioner and president of the Park Board, and it stands as a monument to his good judgment and taste.

The many hundreds of handsome shade-trees and shrubs scattered over the 185 acres of Garfield Park show signs of a healthy growth and form pretty little groves and picturesque groups. The art of the gardener during the summer months transforms a considerable part of the velvety lawns into gorgeous and odorous flower-parterres of various shapes and designs, but the interior of the elegant greenhouse standing in the extreme southwestern corner of the park, is a beauty all the year around. Here Mr. Sell, the head gardener, propagates and cultivates not only the many varieties of bedding plants for outdoor ornamentation, but also some of the choicest species of tropical and exotic plants; especially rich is the collection of orchids, which is quite large and contains some very interesting species of this genus of plants. The park-lake, which covers an area of seventeen acres, and contains two pretty islands, proves one of the main attractions this park possesses. The piazzas of the refectory or refreshment pavilion afford very fine views over lake and parklands and the boat landing directly below with its merry people either embarking for a ride on the smooth water or returning from a trip full of joy and glee.

In 1879 the Illinois Humane Society donated to this park a substantial and beautiful drinking fountain for man and beast. The money for this desirable improvement was contributed by Mrs. Mancel Talcott and the donation was in harmony with the liberal spirit of her late husband, and only one of the charitable acts of the donor.

In May, 1875, permission was given to a number of gentlemen to use the unimproved part of Garfield Park lying south of Madison Street and extending from there as far south as Colorado Avenue as a driving park, but it served this purpose only for a brief period and is now being changed into extensive lawns for base ball, cricket and other outdoor sports, where people, who frequent the park in pursuit of pleasure and recreation, will find increased facilities for satisfying their desires. The present Park Board has in contemplation the erection of a Museum of Natural History in this portion of the park territory and if this plan should be carried out, Garfield Park would certainly then become the mecca of a vastly larger number of people, than have heretofore visited this lovely spot. There is also under consideration the erection of a suitable monument to the memory of our martyr President James A. Garfield, at the Washington Boulevard entrance to the park, and a committee has

Scene In Garfield Park.

been appointed to co-operate with the citizens of the West Division, to secure such a monument, as would be an ornament to the park, and keep alive in the memory of our people the noble traits and character of this distinguished citizen.

Garfield Park is bounded on the North by Kinzie Street, on the East by Central Park Avenue, on the South by Colorado Avenue and on the West by Hamlin Avenue. The artesian well, the water of which contains medicinal properties for stomach and kidney diseases, has a flow of about 150 gallons a minute. The result of an analysis of this water is given on another page of this book

Garfield Park, like all the rest of the parks, will become more and more attractive year by year and the purely artificial will gradually assume its appropriate place in the natural. The location of the parks out on the prairie-land of the West Side has been of inestimable value not only to the City of Chicago as a corporate body, but also to individual citizens, who have profited by large increases of real estate values throughout the surrounding districts; but this has been especially the case in the vicinity of Garfield Park and the avenues leading to it from the city. The actual worth of a plat of land or a building has as truly been increased by the parks being brought to it, as the actual worth of a bushel of corn is increased by its being brought from the prairies of our State to a storehouse in New York. And then look at the business that has been created by the establishment of parks! It has spread so widely in every direction as to be beyond calculation. It may be assumed, for instance, that of the large number of vehicles which enter our parks, nearly one half if not more are hired. The profits of the livery business arising from the use of vehicles for drives to the parks and over our boulevards are shared in small portions by many hundreds or thousands of men, by the owners of the vehicles, the drivers, the stable men, the mechanics who build the carriages and manufacture the harnesses, the breeders who raise the horses and the farmers who produce the hay and grain upon which they are fed. Again the street car companies and even the steam railroads which approach the parks convey each year millions of passengers each way and of the fares they receive about two-thirds must be considered as net profit, for it happens that the tide of travel to and from the parks sets in just at the hours, when there is a lull in the ordinary business transit.

But great as is this pecuniary advantage to the city and to individuals, it is the least of the benefits arising from the parks. Every thing is useful just in proportion as it in some way adds to human enjoyment. A good dinner, a convenient house, elegant furniture, fine clothing, ornaments, a swift horse, or a fast yacht, are useful in this respect and no other. So pictures, statuary and music are useful. In fact, the common distinction between the useful and the ornamental is really baseless. The parks are useful, because they add to human enjoyment. But the amount of enjoyment derived from anything is not unfrequently wholly incapable of being expressed in dollars and cents. If we could find out just how much each of the millions of visitors to our parks would give rather than not have the parks open to them, we could approximate a little toward their value. Even this would be only an approximation, for not unfrequently people derive more benefit than they dream of from enjoyments for which there is no monetary measure. No man can say, for example, how much the health of our city is owing to the parks.

DOUGLAS PARK.

The main drive from the Humane Fountain in Garfield Park to the main drive in Douglas Park is called Douglas Boulevard, which forms an important link in the chain of drives, connecting the three great parks of the West Side Douglas Park, four miles southwest of the Court House, contains 170 acres. The chief beauties of this park are found in its magnificent lake, its beautiful foliage trees, lovely floral decorations and the newly improved section lying south of Ogden Avenue, where, in 1890, a large Palm house, called the Wintergarden, was constructed. This building and its surroundings, although simple in detail, combine to produce an elegant effect and are unique in the park system of Chicago. The Wintergarden is built on an elevation fronting towards Ogden Avenue, about midway between the east and west lines of the park. In this new improvement a large lawn at the southwest end, of sufficient size for amateur ball games, tennis courts and for militia drills, has been laid out. This was thought especially desirable, as heretofore there was no such large lawn in any of the west side parks. South of this lawn is a lake, the excavations from which were used for the necessary filling, as the ground of that portion of Douglas Park was below the grade of the adjacent streets. The lake connects under Ogden Avenue with the older lake to the north of the avenue, and the Wintergarden stands in the midst of terraces, which continue down to the lake to a boat landing at the south. These terraces accommodate quite a large concourse of people, and there is a band stand so placed as to admit a large audience within easy hearing distance. The Wintergarden building is 178 feet long by 62 feet wide at the widest part. It has a center pavilion forty feet square, with wings on the east and west, each wing terminating in an aquilateral cross, the arms being sixty-two feet by thirty feet. The center pavilion is approached from the north and south through wide vestibules, the approach on the Ogden Avenue side containing also the offices of the head gardener, ladies' toilet, the stairs to the basement and to the gallery over the vestibule.

In the center pavilion and in the east wing the plants are mostly set directly into the ground. Here are cultivated the largest tropical plants, such as palms, ferns, banana-trees, etc. The entire improvement, which also embraces a large lily-pond west of the Wintergarden building, was made at an expense of about $60,000.

But the park has many other attractive features. The artesian well in an embowered grotto feeds the lake and is visited by many on account of the medicinal properties of its water, which however is not considered as valuable in that respect as the water from the well in Garfield Park, from where hundreds and thousands of gallons are annually carried away in jugs to private residences throughout the surrounding districts.

From the balconies of the spacious and well equipped refectory is had a fine view of the lake and the most striking vistas of the grounds. Numerous costly improvements have been completed here during the last few seasons among which the new greenhouses erected on California Avenue near Nineteenth Street take a high rank; then the park has been provided with one ladies' and one gentlemen's cottage building and with a band pavilion. The old propagating houses formerly situated near California and Ogden Avenues have been entirely removed and the place laid bare thereby has been transformed into a lawn to be used for floral decorations.

Douglas Park, which was named after the renowned statesman from Illinois, Stephen A. Douglas, is reached by the Ogden Avenue and West Twelfth Street car lines, the distance being about four miles from the Court House.

Residence of Andrew Leicht, near Lincoln Park.

A monument to the memory of Stephen A. Douglas will undoubtedly before long become an important link in the chain of attractive features this lovely park possesses.

To the popular superintendent, Mr. Nelson Johnson, and the gardener in chief, Mr. Zapel, is due in a great measure the credit of keeping steadily in view the one object of making the park a pleasure ground, admitting nothing which would interfere with this, prohibiting nothing which would conduce to it, and as mentioned before, the Commissioners have wisely set apart a portion of the newly improved section south of Ogden Avenue for a parade ground, cricket, the "national game" base ball, etc.   The certainty, that upon any day there is access to the green-sward, forms one of the greatest attractions of the park, especially for those, to whom of all others it is for the well-being of the community that the place should be rendered attractive.   The toil-worn artisan, his weary wife and pining children are assured, that on any bright summer or autumn day they will find sward and shade open to them, and their welcome face therefore becomes more and more frequent in the park.

And now in this connection let us measure out full praise to the men, who, from the year 1869 to the present day, have given their time and personal efforts to the grand work of creating and maintaining the great Park-System of the West Side.   From first to last the administration of the West Park Commissioners has been not only pure, but unsuspected, and few residents of our City need be told how much private worth and public spirit is embodied in the men who have faithfully and without pecuniary reward served the people in the capacity of West Park Commissioners.   The honest and capable administration of all of our parks stands in pleasing contrast to many other departments of our public service.

WEST SIDE BOULEVARDS.

At Halsted Street it is where the grand boulevard system of the West Side begins. Pick your way among the shuttling street cars, avoiding the population, which is heavy in that section, until you reach Jackson Street, or rather Boulevard, for a boulevard it became in name something over two years ago through a decision of the Supreme Court. And now it's a boulevard in fact, and one of the finest long drives in the city, famed for its magnificent stretches of roadway. Jackson Boulevard, with its unpretentious gate, flanked on one side by a theatre building, on the other by a typical Halsted Street saloon, stretches away from there as far as the eye can reach. The roadway, forty-four feet wide, smooth as a marble mantel in a parlor, is one of the best bits of asphaltum work in the world. On each side of the street is a parked strip of green running along the smooth asphaltum as regularly as binding on a garment, separating the sufficient sidewalks from the drive. At regular intervals, twenty-five feet apart, trees, young but full of promise, bear pretty if not abundant foliage, and between them at stated intervals are ornamental boulevard lamps on artistic supports. You drive along by rows of houses that are comfortable even if the elegance that you might expect to see on a boulevard is wanting. Right here is where you want to bring your reflective and comparative quality into action and figure it out that not much more than a year ago the boulevard was only a plain, hardworking, every-day street, so rough that the babies were liable to be jolted out of your family carriage during an afternoon's drive. You will be bound to admit that the asphaltum roadway can't be surpassed, and the beautiful foliage and the boulevard appurtenances generally grow more pleasing as you drive along. And occasionally you see evidences of the boulevard spirit cropping out in improvements on the old houses, that were good enough for a "street," but were thought shabby for a boulevard. Here and there on each side you come upon a new residence that causes you to appreciate the fact that the boulevard spirit has been perfected. For there are residences, new ones, that are models. At every cross street we see evidences of airs being taken on in the way of improvements, and by the time Ashland Avenue is reached and crossed you are convinced that nothing can beat Chicago and its roadways. At that point, as you look west, the trees and the lamp posts begin to come together far away, and Jackson Boulevard seems to have an end in a yellow house with green blinds, and you gain the impression that you have struck a blind boulevard. But you keep on and you see your error, and at the same time a little bit of platting that you will find only in Chicago. Beautiful "winding ways" are often seen, but a boulevard with a right angle curve in it is something entirely Chicagoesque. A long time ago people who owned prairie land out there concluded that the turnpike down to the city would never need to run further than Hoyne Avenue, so somebody built a house right across the road. His heirs and the heirs of his neighbors to the west hold the property, and when the course of empire got to Hoyne Avenue it had to go north a few feet and turn a corner, and so Jackson Boulevard comes to have an angle in it.

But it does not affect it, for it's rather refreshing to swing around the corner, for you come on to a continuation of the boulevard stretching away to the west, beautiful as ever, with its foliage and manor swards of green. The end comes at the portion of Garfield Park south of Madison Street, which is now in the hands of the landscape artist and the workmen. The old trotting

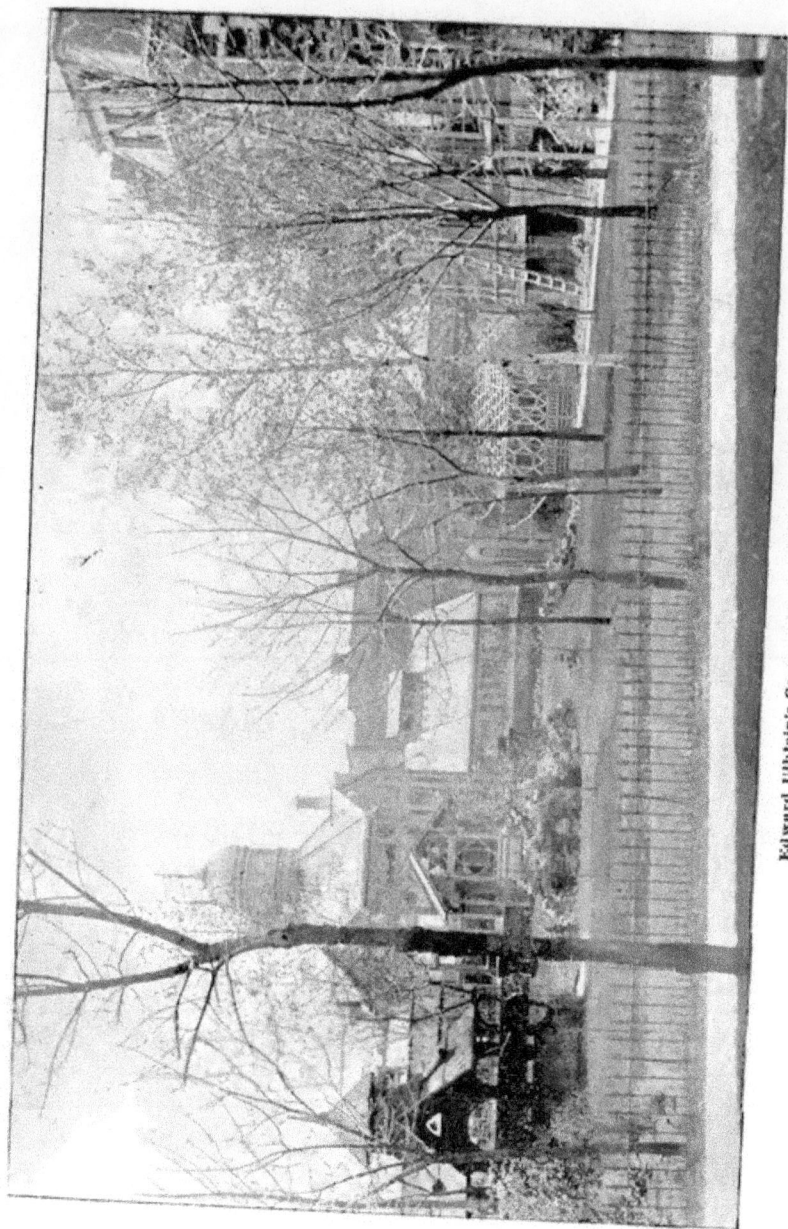

Edward Uihlein's Conservatory, near Wicker Park.

track has been torn up, and it will be the work of but few months to convert
the present unsightly field into a splendid recreation ground for the people.
It will include a speed track for horsemen, tracks for wheel riders and other
special features for the entertainment of patrons. It is indeed a beautiful sight
to look down the beautiful boulevard, behold the enterprise, and to view the
general improvement about its western terminus. But you can't go further
west just now without crossing the improvements under way, so turn the rig
around, or "right about face," and enjoy again the ease of Jackson Boulevard
back to the fashionable thoroughfare of the West Side—magnificent and
stately Ashland Boulevard, whose only fault is that there is not enough of it
between Lake and Twelfth Streets, which mark its termini.

Ashland Boulevard really begins at the north end of Union Park, but the
few blocks of it that skirt that pretty little breathing place are generally considered as a part of the park, and the broad boulevard begins where it is
crossed by Madison Street, which stretches away to the east and west, the
most imposing retail business thoroughfare in the West. To Ashland Boulevard there is neither beginning nor end so far as its stateliness is concerned.
It is as wide as Michigan Boulevard and its roadway is much superior to the
South Side drive so famed and popular. The parking of the boulevard is
tasteful, and the general outlay of the thoroughfare is on a scale of magnificent distances. First one sees from Madison Street the massive Third Presby-
terian Church, and across a triangle from it rises, at the junction of Monroe
Street, Ogden Avenue and the boulevard, the pretty church of the Fourth
Baptist congregation, one of the most striking buildings in all Chicago. The
contrast in these two edifices is only a hint of the variety in architecture and
design that is encountered as the drive along the boulevard is pursued. Ashland Boulevard seems to be the one belt in Chicago that the smoke always
avoids. There is not a shadow of uncleanliness there. The white stone houses
that men built before they learned what a monster soft-coal-devouring Chicago
was going to be, are as immaculate as when they were erected. To the left
in driving north after crossing Monroe Street, one comes on the white-fronted
buildings of the Illinois Club—real swell, and much the same to the West
Side that the Calumet is to the South Side. Across the broad street stands a
row of fine houses resting under the shade of great trees. It's always so
white, this row of houses, that it has come to be known as "ghost row." The
houses are of the old swell front, high-stoop style. They lack the modern,
but they do look so comfortable and respectable, that one keeps on thinking
well of them, even when the great and striking mansions that, in spacious
grounds, line the boulevard further south, bid him stop in admiration.

A characteristic of Ashland Boulevard is that every inch of ground has
not yet been given up to brick and stone. Its chief charm, indeed, is, that
distance prevails everywhere. The houses are not glued together. All of the
great mansions have settings of their own, great green yards with grav-
eled walks and drives and flower beds and shade trees, with lots of room for
the children, for lawn tennis devotees, and for fresh air. The style of architecture prevailing in the latest improvements on the boulevard is massive, but
there is no crowding.

Where Jackson and Ashland Boulevards cross is a beauty-spot. Carter
H. Harrison lives there in a house that is old and out of date, but one sees so
little of the house, and the surroundings are so stately, so comforting, that
one wonders how the owner could cherish an ambition for any other pleasure
than simply living there in the old house. So Ashland Boulevard runs its
course with beauty, elegance, variety and spaciousness on every hand, improving from end to end. That it is in great favor as a driveway, one learns
as he picks his way along its crowded asphaltum pavement on a summer
evening, and dodging here and there, and everywhere wheelwomen who seem
to find in Ashland Boulevard the choicest place of any for their invigorating
recreation. There is much to see in the way of elegant streets from the Boulevard besides its own residences and stately edifices. From the drive one
has a view of these eminently respectable and staid home streets, Adams, Monroe, Van Buren and Harrison, and of marvelously developing Polk and Taylor Streets. To the left, one sees the "medical" district, from the center of

which one sees the buildings that constitute the County Hospital. Surrounding them he sees the medical colleges, private hospitals, schools and other public buildings. But all too soon Ashland Boulevard comes to an end, and Ashland Avenue continues on its course, still a good average street, far beyond the stock-yards, where it is finally lost in the prairies. As the end comes, one looks back with admiration on the broad road, with its regular trees, its pretty lamps and its wide sidewalks, separated from the broad roadway by the smooth greensward; and there is a regret that there is only a mile of the boulevard. The avenue should be asphalted further south than Twelfth Street, and this will probably be done.

But there is consolation to the summer evening-outer, for at Twelfth Street he leaves Ashland Boulevard for another grand drive—maybe not so beautiful as to all its surroundings, but certainly most inviting. Twelfth Street is one of the city's wonders. The stranger who turns on to it from the Ashland Road is amazed, for right at that junction he becomes impressed with the wonderful versatility of the "marvel city." For Twelfth Street Boulevard is democratic. One can find everything there. The asphaltum pavement in the center, wide and smooth as any in the country, is perfectly parked for an even mile. On either side of it run street-car tracks and traffic roads paved with blocks. These are separated from the boulevard proper by plats twelve feet wide, bearing small but splendid trees, from the foliage of which, when they have grown, shade will be cast alike on the equipages that are entitled to roll along the smooth drive and on the humble yellow street-cars, laden with hardworking people, that toil along on either side. There are no angles on Twelfth Street Boulevard It is laid out with beautiful lines. The curbs are rounded. At the street intersections the parks between the drive and the traffic roads come to no abrupt angular ends. They terminate in curved inclosures, and this plan constitutes one of the most pleasing features of the boulevard. The sidewalks are wide and the greensward that lines the edge of the pavements of the other city boulevard is also found on Twelfth Street. The sidewalks are also lined with young trees planted regularly, giving four rows of trees that make attractive lines of green from Ashland Boulevard to Oakley Street. Twelfth Street Boulevard is not a residence thoroughfare. Neither is it a business street. It's a people's road. It is lined with business buildings in the main, but a portion of every building is given up to homes. The buildings, or at least such of them as have been erected since Twelfth Street took on boulevard airs, are modern, substantial, and of unending variety. No business in particular is in the ascendency. Everything is, of course, on the retail plan. Dry goods stores, groceries, meat markets, beer saloons, undertaking establishments, and all other conceivable enterprises flourish side by side. What few structures there are along the line devoted to strictly home purposes are of unpretentious mien. Indeed, a good many of them are shabby, but that there is a pride among the residents is demonstrated by the constant swish of the paint brush and the broom. For everything along the boulevard is as scrupulously clean as the little thatched cot of the poem that school children weep over. There are more children on Twelfth Street Boulevard than on any other in the city, and they enjoy the street. They come from the narrow, unimproved, and in many instances miserable streets that intersect the wide-stretching boulevard, which is their park and playground. They drive their goats and dogs hitched to their box—many of them soap-box—carts about, fully as happy and equally as healthy as their neighbors on the more aristocratic streets. The drive makes everybody equal, for its beauties are as free and accessible to the man who is driving along in charge of a sawdust cart or a coal wagon on one of the traffic roads as they are to the person who lolls on luxurious cushions in a carriage on the wide stretch of asphaltum. Twelfth Street Boulevard is the people's highway. It's as big as the people. It is by far the widest road in town, and to the eye it is the most stately, even though it lacks imposing architectural surroundings found on other boulevards. And to one who reflects and compares there come wonderful manifestations of the achievements of Chicago's dash and progress. The improvement has been of an amazing quality and a lasting quality. And if one sighs for the spice of life, variety, he can get it by looking either way from the boule-

Residence of West Park Commissioner Hermann Weinhardt.
near Wicker Park.

vard and see the loveliness and slovenliness with a single glance. From the head of the boulevard which turns into Ogden Boulevard at Oakley Avenue one can look back and through the great expanse of the boulevard into old Twelfth Street—a narrow business and retail street. Looking west the street runs on wide as the boulevard portion of it, seemingly, to the horizon. Rising from it on either side are buildings everywhere—and substantial ones at that. All that part of the street will come in for improvements some day. Where Twelfth Street Boulevard, Ogden Avenue and Oakley Avenue come together there is an excellent view. One can look miles either way on Oakley Avenue, gaze down between the stretch of busy stores on Ogden Avenue that ten years ago was an unpaved road with uneven sidewalks, and see at the same time two boulevards—Ogden Avenue and Twelfth Street.

Ogden Boulevard runs to the southwest from Twelfth Street Boulevard. It is planned on exactly the same lines as the latter, of which it really is a continuation. About the first thing to attract on Ogden Avenue Boulevard, outside of its own stateliness and evidences of improvement, is the great viaduct that carries the boulevard over a number of railroads and over scores of puffing locomotives and jingling freight trains that seem to be moving at that point at all hours. The Ogden Avenue viaduct is a great piece of engineering. It is a light and airy structure to the eye. But it is as strong as steel and iron can be wrought together by human skill. At the same time it carries a most pleasing appearance and one of safety and endurance. The asphaltum of the boulevard will be laid in the middle bed of the viaduct, while the traffic roads, street-car tracks, and sidewalks will be carried along just as they are on the level streets, save that there will be winding approaches. The approaches to the viaduct are of easy grade, and when they are completed they will be quite artistic. One taking a drive along the boulevard can stop on the viaduct long enough to see Chicago, or a portion of it. As to its industrial features, it is a busy city, as one can see from the tangle of tracks that mean an exit from the city of only a few of its scores of railway lines. The tracks are skirted as far as we can see by great factories of every character. After crossing the viaduct, the boulevard runs up, broad as ever, to the gates of Douglas Park, filled with flowers, and lakes and shade, and winding drives of length sufficient to keep one here traveling over them for an hour, before leaving the park at its western side, and emerging on Douglas Boulevard, which runs west, to connect with the broad road that stretches away for miles and ends in Garfield Park.

Douglas Boulevard from Douglas Park to Garfield Park is one and one-half miles long. As it stands now, it is a right good gravel road, smooth and straight and capable of drawing better speed out of the family horse than the asphaltum roads. The trees are already planted and grown into splendid proportions, a feature that it takes a long time to perfect. There is not much that is novel on either Douglas or Central Park Boulevards. The country is a flat one. But one can see the city crawling up on and filling up the prairie. There are streets platted, and gas lamps, and real estate agents' for-sale signs offering homes.

Crossing West Twelfth Street, one comes upon a lot of red rakish buildings, whence issue cries of agony. Those buildings constitute the city's dog pound, and the cries are from the victims of the dog catchers' brass loops. It's the place of incarceration and death of the city's vagrant dogs. If one has right good eyes he can look far across the country and see the city's home for its petty criminals, the bridewell. Driving north to where Albany Avenue stretches off southwest, Douglas Boulevard passes between the Garfield Park race track, and the new part of Garfield Park proper, which is now in the hands of the landscape gardeners and their forces. Across to the east is the asphalt ribbon of Jackson Boulevard and its lamps and trees. One leaves the rattle of cable cars, and, swinging around a winding road, jostles over the cable road tracks, and finds himself riding along under the heavy shade of the great trees of pretty Garfield Park. If one is going to give time and attention to all the attractions that park contains, with pretty flower beds, its lake, its conservatory, etc., he had better make up his mind to take a day to the task. To traverse its pretty drives and lakes takes a matter of half an hour, and at the end of that time the main gate of the park is reached and before one stretching east is majestic Washington Boulevard, straight as an arrow and ending as it appears in a maze of foliage and church spires. The gates of Garfield Park are attractive and full of welcome. Two roadways lead into it, each diverging from Washington Boulevard and winding their ways around little flower beds.

Two grand residences mark the west end of the boulevard. They are the homes of G. W. Spofford and J. C. Shipley. All the homes on the handsome boulevard are beautiful, but they lose in the features of latter day architecture as you drive eastward toward Union Park. The home of John Eizner, not far from Garfield Park, is one of the latest in design and originality.

Washington Boulevard has cottages too, but they are all in strict accord, in taste if not in dimensions. Everything along the splendid street is built with a view to having its appearance attractive. Even the doctors have taken away the business air of their house fronts, and the face of every building between Union and Garfield Parks tells of home.

Spacious grounds about the residences are not wanting, but the houses are built closer together than on Ashland Boulevard, which it meets at Union Park, one of the smallest, but one of the most attractive breathing spots in the city. The view from the junction of the two beautiful boulevards is grand, with splendid buildings devoted to home, business and religion in several directions, and with the pretty park, its flowers, and its stone bridge and its stone-walled pool in another direction. The administration buildings of the West Park Board occupy one corner of the little park, while near its center is reserved a spot where soon artificially wrought bronze will show the gallant Phil Sheridan on his famous ride to ' Winchester, twenty miles away," a gift of our enterprising fellow-citizen, Charles T. Yerkes.

But our ride is nearly over. You are back at Halsted Street, busy, noisy Halsted Street, four blocks away from the entrance to Jackson Boulevard, where you started on your summer evening's ride but a short time before. You have travelled something like eight miles over perfect roads, and about half that distance over roads nearly perfect. On every hand you have had cause to enjoy yourself and to be impressed with amazement at the marks of improvement, at the magnificence of the boulevards, at the elegance of Chicago homes, of the beauties that are within the city's boundaries, and at the general spirit, enterprise, greatness and grandeur of Chicago. You are refreshed by your outing, full of new information, and altogether glad that you are in Chicago.

The following tables show the length, width and breadth of the West Side Boulevards.

HUMBOLDT BOULEVARD.

				LIN. FEET.	
Width,	250	feet,	from Western Ave. to Logan Square	4,875	4-10
"	400	"	Logan Square	669	
"	250	"	from Logan Square to Palmer Place	2,264	7-10
"	400	"	Palmer Place	1,699	4-10
"	317 250	"	from Palmer Place to North Avenue	3,730	15-100
			Total distance, lineal feet	13,238	65-100
			Total area, acres	90	

CENTRAL BOULEVARD.

				LIN. FEET.	
Width,	400	feet,	from Augusta Street to Grand Ave	890	
"	263	"	" Grand Ave. to Sacramento Square	2,206	5-10
"	400	"	" Sacramento Square	400	
"	250	"	" Sacramento Sq. to Central Park Sq	3,662	6 10
"	400	"	" Central Park Square	400	
"	250	"	" Central Park Sq. to Garfield Park	420	
			Total distance, lineal feet	7,979	1-10
			Total area, acres	47	

Residence of George Rahlfs, Ex West Park Commissioner, near Wicker Park.

DOUGLAS BOULEVARD.

```
Width, 250 feet from Colorado Ave., to Square south of 12th St.  4,077
  "    400  "   (of square)........................................  400
  "    250  "   from Square to Douglas Park.................  3,790

              Total distance, lineal feet.....................  8,267
              Total area, acres...........................  50
```

SOUTHWESTERN BOULEVARD.

```
                                                              LIN. FEET.
Width, 250 lineal feet from Douglas Park to east turn..........  2,950
  "    "      "     east turn.................  ...........  870
  "    "      "     from east turn along California Ave., to
      Thirty-first Street....................................  3,921
Along Thirty-first Street to Western Avenue.............  ......  2,267
Western Avenue south to Canal.............................  740

              Total distance, lineal feet.....................  11,148
              Total are , acres......................  ........  75
```

CITY BOULEVARDS.

```
Washington,  66 feet wide...................1.25 miles.
    "        80    "     .................0.875  "
    "       100    "     .................1.        '    3.125 miles.
Ashland     100    "     .....................    "    1.     "
Twelfth Street 70  "     .....................    "    0.89   "
Ogden Ave.   70    "     .....................    "    1.48   "
Jackson      66    "     .................2.52    "
    "        73    "     .................0.25    "
    "        80    "     .................0.75    "    3.50   "

              Total length...............,.........    9.995 miles.
```

MINERAL WELLS.

Each of the three west side parks possesses a most attractive feature in the shape of an artesian well, containing medical properties of a valuable character.

The analysis of the water of these wells, described in a report by chemist J. E. Siebel, is as follows: One wine gallon of water of the Artesian well in Garfield Park contains:

```
Chloride of Magnesium.............. ...............   8.352 grains.
Chloride of Sodium.....................................  87.491   "
Bromide Magnesium.....................................   0.301   "
Sulphate of Lime.......................................  21.114   "
Carbonate of Lime......................................  14.802   "
Carbonate of Iron......................................   0.712   "
Sulphate of Soda.......................................  13.645   "
Silicate of Soda.......................................   0.508   "
Alumina ...............................................  traces,  "
Organic Substances and Sulphuretted Hydrogen ...........  none.   "

    Total.............................................146.925 grains.
Free Carbonic Acid...............................  13.44 cubic inches
Temperature at the well...........................  71.4 ° Fahrenheit.
```

This water not only contains the largest amount of solid substances of any of the mineral waters in this neighborhood, but it also contains them so arranged and in such quantities that it cannot fail to prove of great benefit in a variety of cases. While its principal character is that of a Saline Water, it still contains a sufficient amount of Iron to allow of its being classified as a

Chalybeate Water in consequence of which its use is indicated in cases in which anæmia is a prominent feature. The saline and calcic properties of the water warrant its use in special cases of indigestion, diseases of the urinary organs, rheumatism, and kindred afflictions. The complex character of the water will be found specially useful in complicated cases, the disposition of which must of course be left to the practicing physician, and in this connection the presence of Bromide of Magnesium will also be considered an important factor. Technically speaking this water is also a Thermal Water, as its temperature is above the mean annual temperature of Chicago, a feature which may also be of some significance at a future day when the subject of public bath houses will receive more attention.

One wine gallon of water of the well in Douglas Park contains:

Chloride of Magnesium	8.236	grains.
Chloride of Sodium	2.320	"
Sulphate of Soda	28.321	grains
Sulphate of Lime	6.422	"
Carbonate of Lime	11.149	"
Carbonate of Iron	0.103	"
Silicate of Soda	0.731	"
Alumina	traces.	
Sulphuretted Hydrogen	faint traces.	
Organic Substances	none.	

Total	57.282	grains.
Free Carbonic Acid	10.22 cubic inches.	
Temperature at the well	57.1° Fahrenheit.	

This water, although in point of general medicinal usefulness it is not equal to that of Garfield Park, will nevertheless be found beneficial in special cases. The calcic character of the water is modified by the predominance of Soda Sulphate, in which this water differs from that of most other Artesian wells. These proportions, together with the small amount of Iron which the water contains, will recommend the same to the attention of thoughtful physicians.

One wine gallon of water of the well in Humboldt Park contains:

Chloride of Magnesium	7.702	grains.
Sulphate of Soda	23.211	"
Sulphate of Magnesia	4.132	"
Sulphate of Lime	10.229	"
Carbonate of Lime	12.131	"
Carbonate of Iron	0.065	"
Silicate of Soda	0.763	"
Alumina	traces.	
Sulphuretted Hydrogen	faint traces.	
Organic Substances	none.	

Total	58.233	grains.
Free Carbonic Acid	11.13 cubic inches.	
Temperature at the well	63.5° Fahrenheit.	

The composition of the water at this well is similar to that of the Douglas Park well, but the amount of purgative salts is less, and their action is counteracted by the presence of larger quantities of Sulphate of Lime. It also contains less Iron than Douglas Park water.

Residence of E. S. Dreyer, near Lincoln Park.

LIST OF WEST PARK COMMISSIONERS.

The following Commissioners have been appointed by the Governor from the origin of the West Chicago Park Board up to the present time:

NAMES OF COMMISSIONERS.	Date of Commissions.		Terms.
Philetus W. Gates*	April	20, 1869	1 year
Henry Greenebaum	"	20, 1869	3 years
Charles C. P. Holden	"	20, 1869	2 "
Clark Lipe*	"	20, 1869	7 "
Isaac R. Hitt	"	20, 1869	6 "
Eben F. Runyan	"	20, 1869	5 "
George W. Stanford	"	20, 1869	4 "
David Cole*	July	15, 1869	8 months
David Cole*	March	1, 1870	7 years
Charles C. P. Holden	February	28, 1871	7 "
Henry Greenebaum	March	21, 1872	7 "
Emil Dreier	"	19, 1873	2 "
George W. Stanford	"	19, 1873	7 "
Eben F. Runyan	"	5, 1874	7 "
Alden C. Millard	April	24, 1875	7 "
Louis Schultz	"	24, 1875	2 "
Clark Lipe*	March	1, 1876	7 "
J. F. Adolf Muus*	September 30, 1876		4½ "
Willard Woodard*	October	8, 1877	7 "
S. H. McCrea*	"	8, 1877	2 "
Peter Schüttler	"	11, 1877	4 months
Emil Wilken	"	11, 1877	5 years
Sextus N. Wilcox*	"	11, 1877	6 "
E. E. Wood	"	11, 1877	4 "
John Brenock	"	20, 1877	4 months
John W. Bennett	November 24, 1877		2½ years
John Brenock	March	2, 1878	7 "
George Rahlfs	"	6, 1879	1 year
S. H. McCrea*	April	24, 1879	7 years
George Rahlfs	March	1, 1880	7 "
Consider B. Carter	April	19, 1881	7 "
J. Frank Lawrence	July	8, 1881	2 "
Harvey L. Thompson	March	1, 1882	7 "
Patrick McGrath	February	15, 1883	1 month
Patrick McGrath	May	8, 1883	7 years
David W. Clark	August	15, 1883	3 "
Christian C. Kohlsaat	November 26, 1883		4½ "
H. S. Burkhardt	March	7, 1884	7 "
Christoph Tegtmeyer, Sr.*	"	12, 1885	7 "
George Mason	"	6, 1886	7 "
Willard Woodard*	April	19, 1886	6 "
Fred. M. Blount	"	22, 1887	7 "
Christian C. Kohlsaat	March	26, 1888	7 "
Harvey L. Thompson	April	20, 1889	7 "
C. K. G. Billings	"	20, 1889	10 months
C. K. G. Billings	March	19, 1890	7 years
John Kralovec	May	10, 1890	5 "
H. Weinhardt	March	18, 1891	7 "
J. L. Fulton	May	22, 1891	9 months
J. L. Fulton	March	24, 1892	7 years

* Deceased.

Voices from the Field of the Dead.

Translated from the German of Karl Gerok, by E. F. L. Gauss.

1. Pet. 1. 24.

For all flesh is as grass
And all the glory of man as the flower of grass.

As in a dream while lost in meditation
I came upon this garden's desolation ;
Who owns this field, this verdant soil I tread ?
—" The dead."

Why tarriest thou, my foot, before this wicket ?
Behold the blooming flowers in plat and thicket !
Whence comes this fragrance rising in sweet waves ?
—" From graves."

See here, oh mortal, where thy paths are ending,
Though snake-like through the world their course they're wending,
It rustles at thy feet midst waste and rust :
—" In dust ! "

Where are they all, men's ever changing chances,
The fickle fortunes which this earth advances ?
These crosses preach the fact to every eye :
—" Gone by ! "

Where are the hearts which in their days' brief measure
So faintly beat in grief, so high in pleasure ?
Which once so ardently by love and hate were swayed ?
—" Decayed ! "

Where are the thoughtless who with health were brimming
And through this world like butterflies were skimming ?
What lies here covered by these mossy stones ?
—" But bones ! "

Where are the strong ones who through life were scouring,
And heavenward their haughty schemes were towering ?
With croaking voice the ravens cry it flurried :
—" They're buried ! "

Where are the dear ones whom, when death did sever
Love swore their memory should last forever ?
The cypress-trees the answer have begotten :
—" Forgotten ! "

And saw no eye which way all those are thronging ?
And spans the grave not the most fervent longing ?
The gloomy firs, lo, shake their crowns forever :
—" No, never ! "

The evening winds in anguish I hear screaming,
My spirit lulls in melancholy dreaming,
The sky grows dim, its glow sends the last ray :
—" Away ! "

Gardens of the Dead.

Entrance Gate to Graceland.

CHICAGO'S CEMETERIES.

INTRODUCTORY.

From ancient times to the present day the burial places of the dead have received much tender care on the part of the living among all civilized people. The decoration of the graves that contain the bodies of dear relatives or famous persons, speaks of the attachment, love and veneration still felt for those slumbering there and these outward signs of love were, in olden times, especially prominent and characteristic marks of human feelings and indicated the degree of civilization of the various nations and communities. It is a great pleasure, though it be mingled with sadness, to give ourselves up for a short time to quiet reveries at the grave of a dear friend or relative and to bestow upon its mound that loving regard which is prompted by the truest and most unselfish love the human heart is capable of.

Much attention is given in Europe to the tasteful arrangement and adornment of cemeteries, but America has made such rapid and marked progress in this direction within the second half of the present century that at present our own country stands unexcelled in point of beauty of burial places, that surround the various cities of the Union. The art of landscape-gardening has been rapidly advanced by the application and opportunity offered by our great park systems and thereby the cemeteries have chiefly profited. This is especially seen in the improvements going on in the older "cities of the dead," where the clumsy fences and similar unseemly enclosures around single graves or lots are rapidly giving way to the "lawn" or "park system," which gives these places a more cheerful appearance. There are of course people who consider a grave-yard full of gloom produced by deep shades of dense trees and bushes and hedges monotonously intersected by long and rigidly straight paths and roads, though it be otherwise entirely void of landscape beauty, the proper place for the burial of the dead. These people are of the opinion that a cemetery ought in all of its appointments and surroundings correspond to the inner sorrow of the mourner and impress him with its gloom never to be forgotten. But, why should this be? Is it not a beautiful and prominent trait of the human character to comfort fellow-men when sorrows overtake them, and lift them up from the dark earth pointing out to them the bright heavens above? If that is charity, it is duty. Is it not the duty then of the managements of cemeteries also to do what is in their power, to make the visits of people who mourn the loss of a parent, child or relative to the graves of the latter less sad, to turn the sorrowful pilgrimage into a source of comfort? We know—alas, a great many of us from personal experience!—that the grief and sadness filling the hearts of men when their loved ones are taken away from them by grim death, lose a great deal of their bitterness and sting, if at the time when we visit their cherished graves, our way takes us through a place with pleasant green lawns, with sweet flowers clustering here and there, where the beautiful sun of the heavens is permitted to spread his golden beams over the graves and their flowers, where the *grave-yard* is not a dark and gloomy and comfortless spot but a place of consolation and peace.

Flowers and blooming shrubs are nowhere more in place than in cemeteries and they are much more appropriate than are costly and pompous memorials of cold stone which are much oftener boasting monuments for the living than the dead. It is true that there are some works of art to be found in our cemeteries, tasteful in style and masterly in execution, but by far the greater number of the monuments are simply towering obelisks with or without urns crowning them. Why these obelisks, which are evidently of Egyptian origin, are so popular in this country is difficult to understand; one might get the impression that the obelisk with the urn is the emblem of the American religion.

In olden times, when the Greeks and Romans and some other nations cremated their dead, the urn was in place, but what meaning it may have in our days, when the remains of man are mostly interred, cannot be comprehended; they certainly do not contain the ashes of deceased persons nor any other relic of them, but are simply blocks of stone in a form that makes them sad reminders of the losses we have sustained. The obelisk itself only impresses by its height and the value of the granite.

Tablets and crosses made of wood are more numerously found within the older cemeteries, especially in many of the "God's Acres" of the Germans. These seem to have been preferred, because the want of space in some burial places makes it necessary to re-sell grave lots after a given number of years. The fact is a sad one that we should not be allowed to remain undisturbed in our last resting place, and some times the inevitable is brought to our notice with painful emphasis. It has only lately transpired, that the son of an old German veteran, who was buried some years ago in a Lutheran cemetery near this city, was looking in vain for his father's grave to erect a monument upon it. At last the management of the cemetery had to admit that it had sold the lot in question to other people.

Happily such cases are not met with in any of our large and beautiful "Gardens of the Dead"; what the future, however, will bring forth and what disposition will be made of the cemeteries when the living shall demand the space occupied by them at present, is a matter of conjecture and a question which we will not attempt to answer

Graceland.—Monument of Frederick and Catharine Wacker.

EARLY HISTORY OF CHICAGO CEMETERIES.

Prior to 1835 this city had no stated place for the interment of the dead.
Up to that time the friends and relatives of the deceased buried them in some
convenient spot near their homes. Then, as time passed, the people living
near the forks of the river, had a common piece of ground, where they buried
their dead. The bodies from old Fort Dearborn mostly found a resting place
north of the main river and east of the old dwelling in which John Kinzie
lived. Here too, the latter was buried in 1828, but in 1835 his bones were dis-
interred and removed to the North Side cemetery, which was situated where
to day the north side pumping station is standing, but even there they found
no rest, for in 1842 they were again taken up and transferred to the Lincoln
Park Cemetery, from where they were removed to their last resting place in
Graceland.

In 1832 there was a small burying ground near the northwest corner of
Wabash Avenue and Lake Street and there the soldiers, who died of cholera
in that year, were interred. Quite a number of deceased persons were buried
along the banks of both branches of the river and it frequently happened in
later days, that the workmen employed in excavating came across forgotten
graves, without being able to ascertain, whose remains the mouldering coffins
contained.

In the summer of 1835, the official surveyor of the town was commissioned
to select and survey two pieces of ground that could be used for cemetery
purposes, one of the tracts, situated in the south division of the city, to contain sixteen acres, the other, which was to be established on the North Side,
to have an area of ten acres. These were the first regular cemeteries of Chicago, and they were located as follows: on the south side near what is to-day
Twenty-third Street and the lake shore; on the north side near Chicago Avenue and immediately west of the lake shore. As soon as these grounds were
turned over to public use, interments were prohibited elsewhere within the
limits of the town. The South Side tract served as a burying ground until
the year 1842, and five years later the bodies slumbering there were taken
up by order of the city authorities, and re-interred in the Lincoln Park Cemetery, which in the mean time had been laid out and put to use. This tract,
of which more details are given in the chapter relating to Lincoln Park, contained three thousand one hundred and thirty-six burial lots and was commonly known as the "Milliman tract." Here also the remains interred in the
old North Side cemetery near Chicago Avenue found their next resting place,
but in 1865, when the city council ordered the vacation of this cemetery, they
and all the rest were again dis-interred. The lot-owners were authorized to
select other lots of equal size in any of the newly founded cemeteries in exchange for the lots surrendered in the Lincoln Park tract. At that time Rosehill, Graceland and Oakwoods had been established, and when the two years
had expired, within which the city had to clear the "Milliman tract" of all the
bodies buried there, the city council named the Aldermen Woodard, Lawson
and Wicker as a committee to make the selection for nearly two hundred lot-
owners, who had failed to hand in their claims and whose whereabouts could
not be ascertained.

The bodies were divided among Graceland, Rosehill, Calvary and Oakwoods. In the latter cemetery the city held the title to the entire "Section B,
third Division," which had been purchased and upon the owners of all lots, in this
manner exchanged, were conferred the privilege of obtaining a deed to the
new lot. The Chicago cemetery in Lincoln Park, where the present Alderman
from the twenty-first ward, Joseph H. Ernst, held the position of Sexton for a
number of years, in 1869 passed under the control of the Lincoln Park Commissioners.

GRACELAND.

Before the close of the year 1893 the number of the silent inhabitants of the necropolis *Graceland* will have reached 60,000.

This cemetery is justly famed as one of the finest among Chicago's cities of the dead, and occupies a similar rank here as does Greenwood Cemetery in Brooklyn, Spring Grove in Cincinnati, Forest Hill or Mount Auburn in Boston. Among the 500 cemeteries in this country there is but a small number that can compare with Graceland in point of beauty of landscape and the splendor of its monuments. But the greatest of the remarkable works, which the art of the landscape-gardener has created there, belong to recent times, to the last 15 years.

At the time when the older sections of this cemetery were first laid out for their present purpose, it was still the fashion to surround the family-lots with low stone walls or fence them in with iron railings or natural hedges and then to adorn them with monuments and grave-stones, more or less gorgeous, as the means of the owners would permit. About 50 acres of the grounds were disfigured in this way. Of course at that time this ancient system had not as yet been recognized as a mistake. That did not become apparent until later on, when the beauties and charms of the park-system created by Strauch had been introduced and welcomed everywhere. But what has thus far been applied of this system at Graceland entitles this cemetery to be termed an ideal burial-ground. We see it well exemplified in the larger eastern half, where Nature, assisted by art, produces alternately solemn and cheerful effects, where the undulating, park-like scenery gives the impression of repose and peace. We see there the chief aim of art is to but modestly indicate what the skillful hand of man can do in artificial and architectural ornamentation, and to leave the main work and effect to Nature itself.

The principal charm of "new Graceland" is found in the large rolling lawns, which appear as grand velvety green carpets, from which the blooming decorations of the low mounds dotting the lawns here and there stand out like many-colored embroideries. Nothing can be compared with the impressive simplicity, which is seen in this serio-bright picture, neither the stately trees with their heavy foliage, nor the well-kept shrubbery throwing their shades over the resting places of the dead, nor yet the bright-blooming flowers and grasses covering the graves, moistened by the dews of heaven or the tears of the mourners. It is the earnest purpose of the present managers of the cemetery to check the excesses in the decoration of burial places so extensively practiced, and to convince the people, that overdoing things in this direction only tends to show to the world the wealth left by the deceased, but is no indication of good taste.

An effort is also to be made to convince people of the impropriety of geometrical flower-beds upon lots; they are not in keeping with the sanctity of the place, but rather remind one of a pleasure-garden. In short, the rules laid down for the park-part of Graceland show the intention of the management not to permit any longer the close erection of monuments and grave-stones nearly alike in size and form, nor the erection of monuments of too great a height.

A very commendable advance in the general embellishment of this cemetery, and one worthy of imitation, has of late been noticeable in the southeastern portion, where the single graves are found. In this part in recent times many graves were seen — as is alas! the case also in other cemeteries —

Scene in Graceland Cemetery.

for which in years no one had cared and which therefore were covered with high grass and weeds and in every respect showed the greatest negligence. The flowers and the obvious care that had been bestowed on some of the other graves by loving hands, only made this wild disorder the more noticeable. These graves, forgotten by the living and allowed to go to ruin by them, have now been cleared of the weeds and grass covering them by the management; the mounds have been levelled and the whole has been changed into a beautiful lawn, on which appear here and there the tops of small numbered stones, marking the resting-places of the dead. This together with the care given to the other graves by loving hands, conveys to the whole the character of a flower-garden, divided up into small sections, and the shade-trees and bushes lend it the additional characteristics of a park. The greatest similarity to the gardens of the living is found in the north-eastern part of the cemetery, where the landscape is embellished by a fine lake with a wooded island in the centre and surrounded on all sides by fine trees and blooming shrubs. In the immediate neighborhood of the lake are the most expensive family-lots, which are in great demand. They are grouped in "sections" and are given such names as "Lakeside," "Bellevue," "Fair Lawn," "Maplewood," "Ridgeland" and the like. They have all been given undulating surfaces, which, together with the beautifully bright-green lawns showing good and constant care, attract the wealthy buyers. Here ground is sold at a dollar to a dollar and twenty five cents per square foot, and as the family lots in this neighborhood contain from 5000 to 12,000 square feet, only persons blessed abundantly with this world's goods can think of buying. The "brotherhood in riches" is one of the chief requirements to obtain a family-lot, but the same condition we also find in other cemeteries. The prices of lots in the leading cemeteries about New York, Philadelphia and Boston range from $1.50 to $5.00 per square foot. It is sometimes regretted that man is dependent even in death upon the prices asked for land, and that people of small means must content themselves with burial places in the out of the way corners of the cemeteries. The adage, that in death all are equal, is therefore not true. But there is another way of looking at the matter. If a cemetery as a whole is considered as a work of art, the broad stretches of lawn, the grand spreading of trees and the beautiful quiet vistas that can only be preserved where there are very large lots, add a value to even the smallest lot.

Near the centre of the cemetery stands the new chapel not long since completed. It is in the gothic style of architecture and the whole building is reared in rich colored Wisconsin granite, whilst red tile cover the roof. The north half of the chapel has a red tile-floor and is supplied with long cushioned pews, whilst the south half is filled with beautiful plants and ferns. The ceiling and walls are decorated with fresco-paintings in harmony with the bright and pleasing color of the benches, doors and wainscoting, which are all constructed of oak finished in natural color. In the middle of the floor is an oblong drop-door through which the coffin is lowered after the funeral services. The lower rooms, partly built under a hill, contain the heating apparatus, a coal-magazine and the vault proper, on the sides of which there are 298 receptacles for coffins. These receptacles are constructed entirely of heavy slate-plates.

Much care has been spent upon the immediate vicinity of the chapel. Few persons would guess that the fine elms which give so much dignity and grace to this building were planted as late as the year 1889. The largest of these is about 60 feet in height, and has a trunk of 2½ feet in diameter. It is believed that this tree is the largest one that was ever transplanted up to that time, but since then a still larger tree has been moved a long distance and planted in Graceland. The abundant foliage with its dark green color shows that these trees have taken a good hold on the soil and are quite at home in their new locations.

Besides numerous elaborate monuments Graceland has also many private vaults which are however, aside from a few exceptions, no ornament to the cemetery. The exceptions are the vaults more recently erected. These are

5

built entirely above ground under the direction of the management and are embellished by artistic decorations of real merit, for other ornaments are no longer suffered at Graceland. The praiseworthy exceptions are led by the vaults of Martin A. Ryerson, Henry H. Getty, William H. Mitchell and those of the Huck and Schoenhofen families.

The first person buried at Graceland was Daniel Page Bryan, who had first been laid to rest in the old city grave-yard (now Lincoln Park), but was afterwards disinterred with about 2,000 others and buried at Graceland. It may also be mentioned, that the original charter of the Company, granted in 1861, was in 1865 amended to the effect that 10 per cent of all receipts from the sale of lots must be turned over to the trustees to form a permanent fund for the purpose of keeping the cemetery in order.

Graceland Cemetery was established to meet the necessities, which a general demand for extramural interments had created. Thomas B. Bryan, in 1860, purchased the eighty acres of land, which to-day comprise the principal portion of the beautiful grounds and in the year following the Legislature conferred upon Mr. Bryan, William B. Ogden, Edwin H. Sheldon, Sidney Sawyer, Geo. P. A. Healy and others the power to incorporate as the "Graceland Cemetery Company," of which the five persons named constituted the first board of managers. The act granted to the company the privilege of acquiring a tract of land to be used for cemetery purposes, not to exceed five hundred acres.

The first president of the board, Mr. Bryan, remained in office until 1865, when he was succeeded by James L. Reynolds, but at the expiration of the latter's term, Mr. Bryan again assumed the duties of the office from 1868 to 1878, after which time, Thomas E. Patterson was elected president, and he held that office for a term of three years. Then Bryan Lathrop became president, which office he has since filled in a manner highly creditable to himself and his fellow-members of the board; besides being president, he also is the treasurer of the company, which made a wise move when it procured the valuable services a number of years ago of the well known landscape architect and cemetery superintendent Mr. O. C. Simonds, to whose skill and good taste may be ascribed many of the natural beauties and fine landscape effects this cemetery is justly renowned for.

After the organization of the company in 1861, it acquired forty-five acres west of the original section, then, three years later, five acres east of it and in 1867 the entire territory was increased by one hundred and nine acres more, which were situated north of it. At that time the Legislature was induced to pass a law, confining the area for cemetery purposes to eighty-six acres, the section improved. This measure precipitated long and weary complications, which were not adjusted until the year 1879. Then the limits of the cemetery were fixed as follows: Green Bay road on the west, Stella Street on the east, Sulzer Street on the north and Graceland Avenue on the south.

The cemetery is situated about two miles north of Lincoln Park and is reached by the Chicago and Evanston Railroad, the trains of which land their passengers for Graceland at the handsome depot and office building the cemetery company has erected near the eastern boundary of the grounds; the horse cars, connecting with the Clark Street cable-line at Diversey Street, also lead to Graceland and beyond. The city office of this cemetery is in the Montauk Block, No. 115 Monroe Street.

Entrance to Rosehill.

ROSEHILL.

One of the largest and most **beautiful** of the cemeteries surrounding **our** city is *Rosehill.* It contains within its enclosure 300 acres of ground, but may be enlarged at any time when it becomes necessary to 500 acres. The grounds were dedicated on July 28th, 1859, **which was an** occasion of no **small** significance.

Rosehill is situated 6½ miles north of the Court house, and **is reached** either by the Green Bay Road **or the** Chicago and North Western **Railroad.**

At the time when this cemetery was laid out many of the **100,000 in-** habitants our city had then considered the distance from it much **too great—** but yet, **even** the people **who had** originally laid **out** the old city grave **yard** (now Lincoln Park) **were found** fault with for locating it too far out **of the city.** Yet it took very **few** years before the growing city put its monster **arms around** it and it became necessary to dig out the remains of those laid to **rest there** but a short **time** before and to transfer them to cemeteries further **distant—the** dead had to give way to **the** living. And to-day again circum- stances are taking the same turn **once** more, for Rosehill, St. Bonifacius, Graceland, the German Lutheran cemetery and two Jewish burial grounds yet further south are now all within the city limits and are surrounded on all sides by human dwellings, which in some locations, *f. i.* in the neighbor- hood of Graceland, are very rapidly growing in number. And how long will it be before **the** cemeteries mentioned, at least the ones nearest the heart of the **city,** will have **to give way** to the living, their necessities and improvements? Nothing will **be able to withstand the** growth of this still young giant—not **even** death.

Rosehill was selected as the general city burial grounds by a committee appointed at the time by the City Council, chiefly on account of its high and consequently dry location, the same being 30 to 40 feet above the level of Lake Michigan, an advantage of great importance in a cemetery.

At the dedication of the cemetery there were present as many **as 8000 to** 10,000 people ; it was conducted under the auspices of the Order of Free- masons. The dedicatory address was delivered by Dr. J. C. Blaney, then the President of the Cemetery Company. Among other remarks, he made the following:

ADDRESS OF DR. BLANEY.

"Ladies and Gentlemen:—You are assembled to-day **to** witness and assist **in the** dedication of this beautiful spot as a rural cemetery. Your presence **here in** such numbers is accepted by those who have undertaken the work as **an** earnest of your interest in their efforts to supply to Chicago that mournful **but necessary** adjunct—A City of the Dead.

The **custom** of burying the dead within **the limits of** large cities **is one** which was **unknown** to the ancients, and **resulted from** the abuse of a privi- lege granted, at **first** only as a mark of high distinction, to martyrs and saints, and afterward claimed as **a right** by the rich and powerful, but **ever** depre- cated by science and by the Church as detrimental to the public health.

By the Jews, the Greeks, and the Romans, cemeteries were by the most rigorous enactments placed without the walls of cities and villages, and this salutary provision **was** adopted in the discipline of the early Christian Church.

It was only during the period of decadence of letters in the Middle Ages **that** this custom, injurious to the living and unwarranted by any principle of public hygiene, by good taste or by respect for the dead, was allowed to creep in as one of many evidences of stolid ignorance and degraded morals. With the revival of letters efforts began to be made to remedy a custom, whose consequences in the more crowded communities of Europe had come to be seriously felt. To the clergy of France, and more especially to the Archbishop of Toulouse, is due the credit of arousing public sentiment to the dangers of intramural interments. In a most eloquent appeal, after rehearsing the abuses by which the practice had been introduced, he portrays vividly the evils to which it gives rise, and exhorts the secular powers to assist the efforts of the Church "to recall the ancient discipline on this point."

It was not, however, until 1765, that the Parliament of Paris, by legal enactment, led the way to a remedy of these evils; the French Government adopted the same course, and those noble institutions "Pere la Chaise," "Vaugirard," and "Montmartre," were the first exemplars of those rural cemeteries which both in Europe and America are at once the ornaments and the patterns of horticultural tastes of so many large communities. I have only to point you to Mt. Auburn, Greenwood, Laurel Hill, Forest Lawn, Mt. Hope, and Spring Grove, as illustrious examples of the disposition in our country to a return to the correct taste and delicate sentiment so beautifully expressed in the epitaph of Sophocles, the founder of Grecian tragedy:

> "Wind gentle evergreen, to form a shade
> Around the tomb where Sophocles is laid;
> Sweet ivy wind thy boughs and intertwine
> With blushing roses and the clustering vine;
> So shall thy lasting leaves, with beauty hung,
> Prove a fit emblem of the lays he sung."

To-day inaugurates a movement in imitation of these examples, and in the citizens of Chicago we look to sustain our efforts.

A brief statement of the history of the enterprise thus far, and of the policy intended to be pursued by the Board of Managers of Rosehill Cemetery, will not be out of place. In the Autumn of 1858, a petition was presented to the Common Council of Chicago remonstrating against the further interment of the dead in the city cemetery.

The gentlemen to whom the matter was referred, proceeded with their duty with commendable zeal and promptness. They opened a correspondence with the authorities of the several large cities of the United States and the Canadas, procuring a vast amount of statistical information and numerous documents. They also made a reconnoisance of the vicinity of Chicago, with a view of effecting a new location for the city cemetery. Among other localities, the one upon which we now stand was examined, and in the unanimous opinion of the committee, was not merely the best, but the only spot in all respects suitable for the purpose.

The report of the committee attracted the attention of several of the gentlemen corporators of the Rosehill Cemetery. The idea of the suitableness of this tract of land for cemetery purposes had previously occurred to them, but until the report was made to the Common Council adverse to the continuance of the city cemetery, the movement was thought to be premature. This report suggested that the time had arrived when the public sentiment of Chicago was prepared to support the efforts which might be made to establish a rural cemetery at a convenient distance from the city limits.

The Board of Managers of Rosehill Cemetery, appointed under the act of incorporation, encouraged by the report of the Committee of the City Council, and feeling bound to supply the need of a place for burial without delay, initiated the preliminaries for the location of the cemetery at this place. With this view they solicited and obtained the eminent counsel of J. Jay Smith, Esq., President of Laurel Hill Cemetery at Philadelphia, who, in view of the importance of the movement to the future health and prosperity of Chicago, sacrificing his convenience and other engagements in an incle-

ment season of the year, visited Chicago and freely gave his assistance in locating the grounds for the future cemetery, and both then and since has been of eminent service by his advice in the management of the enterprise. The Board of Managers would wish thus publicly to express their obligation to this gentleman and their high estimation of his experience in the management of rural cemeteries, and the value of his counsels.

But, fellow citizens of Chicago and vicinity, with you it remains to decide whether Rosehill is or is not to be your cemetery. We have made every effort to supply your need. That effort will be continued, so that you shall not blush to compare yours with the rural cemeteries of other and older cities. But to effect this we must be sustained by your sympathy and encouragement."—

The speaker himself was laid to rest under the leafy roof of the grove, for which he had so great a liking, on the 13th day of December, 1874.

Thirty-four years have rolled down into eternity since that dedication. Then only one person, Dr. J. W. Ludlam, slept the eternal sleep in its grounds, to-day more than 25,000 are resting beneath its green sod, most of them in the old portion of the cemetery, which is nearest the main entrance and comprises 80 acres. West of this old section, in which the erroneous practice of earlier days to fence in graves and lots had taken place, the eye is attracted by the park-like landscape into which that new part has been changed. Here we see plainly the difference between the old and new system. On the one side we behold the irregular mass of grave-stones forming an unsightly chaos with the rusty, partly broken down iron fences, the delapidated and crumbling stone-walls, the wild shoots of grass and the neglected graves, and beyond the bright beauty and symmetry of smooth and green patches of lawn, by which the graves are enclosed and here and there covered. What a difference! How fortunate, that the "old things have passed away and all things have become new!" a comfort indeed upon the field of the dead. And here it may be mentioned that the idea to give grave-yards the character of parks originated with the famous landscape-gardener Adolph Strauch, the creator of the beautiful Spring Grove Cemetery, near Cincinnati, who himself has gone to his rest in the prime of life. Spring Grove Cemetery has ever since its creation by Strauch been the model burial park and is widely copied by landscape gardeners in charge of cemeteries all over the country. The fact that the new system is not without its opponents and enemies speaks loud in favor of it for the world is full of old fogies and obstructionists.

The chief aim in the new part of Rosehill is to come as near to nature as possible in all arrangements and appointments and thereby to produce true landscape effects. This is done without leaving nature entirely to itself, for every one knows what then would become of the wild dame—unrestrained nature soon becomes unnatural. Considerable skill is displayed in the planting of trees and shrubs, giving the cemetery at the same time a cheerful yet solemn appearance. Unfortunately here too the harmony is endangered by the bad tastes of some individual lot-owners, who have begun to disfigure the place by numerous grave-stones and monuments of a similarity in the patterns, that in most cases they differ from each other only in the names of the inscriptions. It is astonishing that the "manufacturers" of grave-monuments content themselves with the everlasting sameness of their productions and cannot summon enough energy and ambition to create something original in their line at least once in a while. Original grave-monuments are indeed the most scarce products of our times. It is as if the obelisks filling the cemeteries everywhere had as so many colossal weeds propagated and promulgated indestructible seed, which had shot up all around. If those inclined to weigh down the graves of their departed by heavy stones and perpetuate—for a time at least—their own names by costly monuments over their tombs, would only entrust the work to real artists, the appearance of our cemeteries would greatly profit and the simple symmetrical beauty of well shaped grave-mounds would no longer be drowned in the flood of unsuitable trash now marring the simplicity, the solemnity and the natural grandeur of these places.

The general character of the western portion of Rosehill cemetery, with its lawn system and natural beauty, shows that the Superintendent of this necropolis, Mr. George H. Scott, knows how to combine effectually the pleasing in the general aspect with the required solemnity of the place, so that comfort is conveyed and yet serious contemplation is awakened. He uses nature and art to excellent purpose. It was in this portion of the cemetery where recently a monument was erected to the murdered millionaire A. J. Snell, an obelisk of course, hewn out of blue Barry Granite, about 50 feet high and costing $12,000.

Of the other monuments in which Rosehill abounds, we will mention only a few of the most costly and largest. The granite obelisk not long since erected to the memory of "Long" John Wentworth, towers considerably above all the others, as Mr. Wentworth himself was during his life time, "a head taller then all the people." The stone shaft including the foundations rises to a height of 65 ft. and is made of Hallowell granite. As we learn from Mr. Chadband, the Assistant Superintendent of the grounds, the Wentworth obelisk has cost $38,000, exclusive of $10,000 expended for and on the lot, on which are planted fifty trees. Nearly $50,000 for a burial lot and a stone monument — not a cent for benevolent purposes! Not by far the most desirable memorial.

The monument to the Volunteer Fire Brigade is a high marble column, crowned by a single figure, representing a fireman on the look-out. Above the foundation which shows representations from the life of firemen on duty upon its four sides, a fire-hose hewn out of marble is wound around the pillar. The corners of the pedestal represent hydrants and the circular patch of lawn in the midst of which the monument stands and which is surrounded by a low stone wall, is adorned with a number of allegorical figures and with flowers.

Not far from this spot is the Soldiers' Monument, a high obelisk. on which stands the stonecarved figure of a soldier of the late civil war. The bas-reliefs on the sides of the pedestal represent the four military divisions: Cavalry, Artillery, Infantry, and the Navy. In front is the inscription: "Our Heroes." On the lawn spreading from the monument is a circle, the Coat of Arms of the United States appears in the bright and living colors of flowers. This monument is opposite the entrance, and east of it on the other side of the carriage road we behold the monument of "*Battery A.*" This consists of a cannon hewn out of stone, covered by the Starry Flag, alongside of it is a pyramid of cannon balls of stone. At the foot appear the names of the fallen members of the battery and those of the battles in which the latter have taken a part. Opposite to this, on the south-east corner of the intersecting carriage roads, we have the stone monument of "*Battery B,*" representing a mortar upon a stone foundation.

Directly east of these Veteran Monuments are two large square plats of lawn, in which 230 Union soldiers are buried. The graves beneath, in which these "defenders of the country" are sleeping, form long straight rows and are marked by low head-stones, upon which are found the names of those resting beneath and of their regiments and companies. Upon not a few however this information is missing and in its place we read only the words: U. S. Soldier. They belong to the large army of the unknown. Not far from the eastern border of these soldier-graves, towards the castle-like gate, towers the obelisk of Gen. Thomas E. G. Ransom.

The monuments thus far mentioned are the most expensive and some of them may lay claim to artistic execution, but others would also call forth admiration, if they were found in a cemetery furnishing resting places to less wealthy people.

As the lot holders in Rosehill Cemetery had become fearful that the cemetery may, after the lots therein shall have been sold, come to be neglected and left without care; therefore, to prevent the possibility of such results, the Rosehill Cemetery Company proposed and adopted the following amendments to its charter:

Rosehill.—Hon. John Wentworth's Monument.

SEC. 1. "Be it enacted by the people of the State of Illinois, represented in the General Assembly, that there shall be set apart and kept, to be reserved and expended as hereinafter provided, the sum of ten per centum, or one-tenth part of all the proceeds hereafter to be received from the sale of lots by the Rosehill Cemetery Company, incorporated by that name by an Act approved February 11, 1859, until the sum so reserved and set apart shall amount to one hundred thousand dollars.

SEC. 2. That the aforesaid sum of one hundred thousand dollars shall be kept and preserved as a fund, for all time to come, for the preserving, maintaining and ornamenting the grounds, lots, walks, shrubbery, memorials, boundaries, structures, and all other things in and about said cemetery and belonging to said corporation, so that the purpose and intention thereof shall be carried out, and so that said grounds shall be and continue as cemetery grounds forever.

SEC. 3. That the said corporation, by its proper officers, shall pay over the said ten per cent. of all sales of lots, from time to time, and as often as they shall be thereunto required, to three Trustees, who are hereby constituted the "Board of Trustees of the Rosehill Cemetery," who shall be owners of lots in said Rosehill Cemetery, and who shall be appointed as hereafter provided, who shall keep the said fund in their possession until a sufficient amount has accumulated to purchase such one of the securities hereinafter provided, as shall be deemed best by the said Trustees, and as often as there shall be sufficient accumulation for the purpose, as above provided. The said Trustees shall invest the said fund in the bonds or securities of the City of Chicago, the bonds or securities of the County of Cook, the bonds or securities of the State of Illinois, or the bonds or securities of the United States, as they shall deem best; or if no such bonds can be had, then in other State securities of the highest value, looking to their safety and the amount of interest to be received therefrom. The said bonds or securities so purchased, shall be at once deposited in the custody of the Mayor and Comptroller of the City of Chicago, as a special deposit—the said bonds having been first plainly endorsed as belonging to the safety fund of the Rosehill Cemetery. The said fund, when so invested, shall be kept and held for the uses and purposes specified in the second section of this Act and no other."

Before we leave Rosehill it is only proper to state that the management of this cemetery pays much attention to the floral embellishment of the grounds, keeping a palmhouse and several hothouses. This gate, too, is remarkable for its characteristic beauty. In this building are found tool-houses in one wing and in the other the office and a spacious and well equipped chapel.

The board of managers consists of Hon. Henry W. Blodgett, H. F. Lewis, Hon. Van H. Higgins, Hon. J. B. Bradwell, and Wm. H. Turner. The officers of the company are: Wm. H. Turner, Vice-President and Auditor, Hon. Van H. Higgins, Treasurer, and Eugene C. Long, Secretary. George Scott is the civil engineer and landscape architect, Walter Chadband the lot salesman, and Thos. Wallis manager of the green-house department.

CALVARY CEMETERY.

The improved taste of late years in the choice of sites for cemeteries and the methods adopted for their embellishment, together with the wide-felt public interest in them, and the laws which guard them from desecration, are certainly very aptly illustrated in Calvary. Here the fact is fully established, that a well-appointed cemetery exerts a reflex influence upon the public taste. Here a large part of the ground is laid out according to the principles of modern landscape art, trees and shrubs are plentiful and they especially have some natural fitness or have become associated with the spot by the usages of the past. Add to all of this the improvements made from year to year, slopes of green velvety lawn, beautiful shade trees and other plants and costly monuments of various designs.

In this cemetery people can learn by personal inspection how beautiful nature is, both in her own simplicity, and when her charms are heightened by the touch of art. And dont say, that such visits answer no purpose save to gratify an idle curiosity! They suggest new ideas; they awaken purer tastes; they show how the simplest piece of ground may be embellished by a little skill and labor; how even the stern repulsiveness of the grave can be chastened; and they send him back to his usual sphere of life determined to adorn his own home, and to beautify the spot where he expects ere long to lay his ashes too.

The fact is significant then and it is honorable to the character of our people, that we are not wholly engrossed in the worship of mammon, neglectful of the amenities and tender charities of life.

There are few who would not, if they could choose, choose such a peaceful place, as Calvary Cemetery, where the great companionship of dead gives a sense of fellowship, sad but not painful. There is no jarring noise of life; no hustle recalling the pain and travail of existence; not even the murmur of the lake close by, or the low breathing of the distant city; its roar being softened here to a whisper.

In Calvary Cemetery we feel that we are face to face in a solemn spot with the old enemy—we are fronting the old, dreadful and incontrovertible fact. The same in all other countries and with every race; we are here in the very presence-chamber of King Dead.

Of course, here too, as is the case in nearly all of our cemeteries, private property in the shape of costly monuments is made more conspicuous than the sentiment of neighborly fellowship or human brotherhood. It is of course proper for every man to express his own taste and judgment, and indeed, speak his own individuality, in the structure and surroundings of his own tomb and that of his family. Father Abraham took the lead in thus doing and his children have followed him with considerable variety of adaptation, as well as marked reverence for his preference for the rock sepulchre over the Greek and Roman urn burial.

It is important for every family to put its own history upon its memorial stone, with as much impression of personal feeling as sober second thought favors and as distinct and just a record as will keep the family name alive for coming generations. But here in this cemetery the aim is also noticeable, to express love for the deceased in such a way that it speaks to every true heart —lifts private sorrow into universal fellowship. Some of the simplest expressions on some of the marble slabs or upright memorials do this, with their solemn prefix: "In Peace" and the name of the dead, and perhaps with a rude figure of the Good Shepard with a lamb in his arm.

Quite a significance is given to this garden of the dead through its long register of heroes, who have given their lives for their country. These soldiers' monuments, among them the one of the gallant and brave Col. Mulligan, are neither too warlike nor fierce in their inscriptions and symbols. They express the fact, that all true heroism approaches the great sacrifice, and should nurture the brave charity that calls all citizens to live under the same liberty and law, and invites all souls into the same divine brotherhood.

The successful attempt has been made in Calvary, to combine as much serious unity of purpose as possible with the variety of the grounds, woods and water, as well as to guard against the too frequent mechanical monotony of enclosures and monuments by favoring all judicious variety of vegetation, landscape and stonework.

It is well to encourage the people in calling attention to the great beauties of their cemeteries and to impress them with their need of a still higher order of memorial art. We believe in nature and the human mind and in our right and duty to know and love all that is good and true and beautiful; this faith we may declare in metal and in marble, in granite, flowers, trees and shrubs upon our graves.

Calvary, as it is at present, forms a picture well worthy of a place in our memory and thoughts. The natural dignity of the landscape, enhanced by the graces of architecture and sculpture, leaves an impression not easily effaced.

Among the chief beauties of Calvary are the great number of forest-trees, evergreens being intermingled with deciduous trees, which together show a harmonizing of the mixture in summer, and in winter the evergreens are lightened and set off by the contrast of the shade-trees bereaved of their foliage, for even the leafless branches of trees and shrubs afford an available element of color.

Of the avenues the one leading from the entrance gate through the cemetery, where it diverges and branches out, is laid out in good taste and possesses great natural charms. All the drives and walks are kept scrupulously clean and the shortcomings in this respect noticed in former years have been supplanted by care and painstaking.

But as pointed out before, the skill and taste of the sculptor and architect have been exerted in a remarkable manner in the construction of elaborate monuments and mausoleums, and while greenhouse flowers and plants embellish numerous graves, the lawns beneath the leafy canopy of elms and ash and maple are, during the warm season, sprinkled with a host of simple and modest flowers of the meadow and forest. These and the fragrant flowers arranged by the florist or planted by lot-owners on the little hillocks are the silent but expressive teachers of morality.

All in all this cemetery has undergone such a vast change in the last few years, that it reflects honor upon the sensibility and taste of the management. Nature has done a great deal for this judiciously located burial ground and art has not been backward in contributing to its embellishment. It is impossible to visit this vast sanctuary of the dead without feeling a solemn yet sweet and soothing emotion steal over the senses, as we wander over these hallowed grounds interspersed so abundantly with luxuriant flowering shrubs and fragrant herbs, that seem to defy the most profane hand to pluck them.

Among the new improvements made during the last few years the new greenhouses built are not only the most prominent, but they also fill a long-felt want. They were erected on the west line of the cemetery, north of the imposing entrance gate and are spacious and well adapted to their use. The building consists of a propagating house, 150 feet long and 19 feet wide, another house of equal dimensions serving also for the cultivation of flowers and plants and a show-house, smaller in size, but filled with beautiful species of palms, rubber plants, cactuses, banana-trees, ferns, etc. At the southern extremety of the plant-house, a commodious waiting room for ladies is provided with which is connected the office of the florist, Mr. M. N. Angelsberg, an adept in floriculture and floral decoration. The two greenhouses contain all the most desirable and beautiful bedding-plants, such as bigonias, geraniums, heliotrop, pinks, pansies, fuchsias, echeverias and countless numbers of other plants, such as are generally used for carpet bedding.

The rose too is cultivated here, because no other flower forms such a beautiful emblem of affection and tenderness. This shrub was early used for grave-yard ornament by the Greeks and Romans, who frequently made it their dying request that roses should be yearly planted and strewed upon their graves. They conceived that this custom had a power over the dead. Anacreon declares that it

> "Preserves the cold inhumed clay,
> And marks the vestige of decay."

How delightful to behold filial affection thus employed in decorating and beautifying the spot where the ashes of a tender parent, a beloved child, sister or brother repose! How pleasing to think, that even here we shall not be forgotten—that our memory will be cherished by those who once loved us, and that the spot where we rest will be sometimes bedewed by the tears of sorrowing love, and decorated by the hand of tenderness—that flowers will fringe the pathways leading to our lowly resting-place.

Among the memorials placed on family-lots there are quite a number that can justly lay claim to high artistic value and refined taste. Besides the monument erected by friends and admirers of the gallant soldier Col. Mulligan, those of Wm. M. Devine, Thomas Lynch, Chas. J. O'Neill, John D. Tully, John Cudahy, Philip H. Murphy, Mrs. John Hogan, John McAvoy, W. B. Snow, David Thornton, etc, are very conspicuous for their elegance. Then there is the handsome and costly family vault erected by Richard M. Hooley, and the P. J. Sexton mausoleum also makes a very fine appearance. Of great artistic value is the monumental sarcophagus for J. A. Wolford and wife, a masterpiece indeed of the sculptors' art.

Not less than 120,000 bodies have been laid to rest in this "Yard of Peace" from the day its grounds were consecrated up to the present time. It is truly a cosmopolitan burying ground, for with the exception of the Chinese perhaps all nationalities are represented here by some one of their own people having been permitted to enter these fields after reaching the end of life's journey. Even an Indian Chief—"Little Thunderer"—is sleeping beneath the green sod of Calvary,

Before Mount Olivet, the Catholic cemetery situated southwest of the city, on the Grand Trunk railway, was established, the daily average of interments at Calvary had reached 15, since then it has been reduced to 14.

The cemetery is located south of and adjoining the village of South Evanston, ten miles north from the City Hall. It is the largest and oldest of the Roman Catholic cemeteries of this city and is fronting Sheridan Drive and Lake Michigan. It is the favorite burying-place of the Irish Catholic Churches and was consecrated in 1859, although prior to this some of the bodies taken from the consecrated ground in the old Chicago Cemetery were re-interred here. The cemetery is a large one, containing 110 acres, which were purchased in the year 1856, by Bishop O'Regan from John Devlin and John O'Leary, Trains of the Chicago & Northwestern Railway (Milwaukee Division), and of the Evanston Division of the Chicago, Milwaukee & St. Paul Railroad stop in front of the handsome gate leading to Calvary.

The money derived from the sale of lots and single graves is turned over to the Archbishop who, as head of the Catholic Churches of this city, manages this fund in the interest of Calvary and Mount Olivet Cemeteries, where from time to time costly improvements become necessary. A large part of this money is kept in reserve for the purchase of additional territory for cemetery purposes, for it is only a question of time and a comparatively short one too, when Calvary will be completely filled with bodies and new fields will have to be opened somewhere in the vicinity of the city for those, who during coming years will throw off the "mortal coil" and go on their last journey to the grave.

The city office of Calvary Cemetery is on the second floor of the Reaper Block, on the northwest corner of Clark and Washington streets. Mr. Thomas Brenan, favorably known to most of our citizens as a gentlemen of unques-

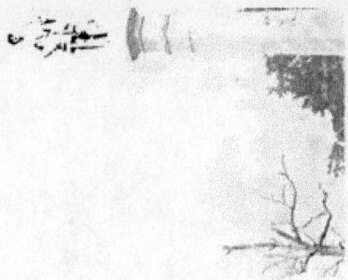

tioned honesty and integrity, who has served the public faithfully for a great many years in various high public offices of honor and trust, is the General Superintendent of Calvary and Mt. Olivet, and as such he acts as the financial and trusted agent of the Archbishop. His able assistants are D. P. Kinsella, who has charge of the cemetery management at Calvary, John Baynes, who serves in a like capacity at Mt. Olivet, and Joseph McLaughlin, Mr. Brenan's valuable adjunct at the main office.

ST. BONIFACE.

The first cemetery we encounter on our return from Rosehill (along the Greenbay Road or Clark Street) is St. Boniface, which, together with St. Mary's, situated southwest of the city, and the Orphan Asylum at Rosehill, is managed by a board of directors composed of members of the following parishes: St. Michael's, St. Joseph's, St. Peter's, **St. Antonius**, St. Franciscus, St. Boniface, St Paul's, St. Augustine, St. Alphons, **St. Aloysius**, St. Martin's, St. Peter and Paul's, St. George's, the Holy Trinity, **St. Mary's**, St. Henry's and St. Mathias.

The cemetery has **an area of 36 acres**, of which ten **acres are not** yet divided into burial lots. **In the new, eastern part** of the cemetery, **the** spirit of progress has plainly manifested **itself, as** the lots laid out there are arranged in accordance with the **park** system **in** vogue now in most burial-grounds. Thereby the difference between the **older** portion in the eastern half of the grounds and this new part becomes very pronounced and at once noticeable and **there** is nothing but praise among the owners of lots in the western portion **concerning** the arrangements, the dispensing with fences or stone-enclosures around **flower-covered** mounds. But in view of the fact, that the old part **with its** regular squares and low stone-enclosures, is kept in excellent order **and** receives the best of **care on** the part of the lot owners and the management, there **is** not much **to** be said against this part either, for the rigid straight lines **are** largely lost sight of through the tasteful floral ornaments or other emblems of mourning produced by nature or the handiwork of man.

This cemetery, upon which many, very many, of our best-known and highly respected German citizens have been laid to rest in their graves, was laid out in 1863 and consecrated the same year. On the 19th of October it received its first silent inhabitant in the person of Marie Jung, a nine-days old infant. To-day there are resting in the cool earth of St. Boniface, 26, 200 bodies, to which are added on an average five each day.

From the stately portal, adjoining which **are the offices of the** Superintendent and Secretary L. Biehl, a beautiful **wide avenue flanked by** stately trees leads straight through the cemetery past **the vault; beyond that** it terminates in several winding driveways, in harmony **with the** park-like nature of that part of the grounds.

St. Boniface cemetery **differs** from most other **burial** grounds, the public, as well as the church cemeteries, in **so far, that the** surplus of the annual receipts are expended for benevolent purposes, especially for maintaining the orphanage at Rosehill, while the often large profits of the other cemeteries, with hardly an exception, find their way into the pockets of single individuals **or** the coffers of corporations.

Take for instance the year before last, in which there were buried in St. Boni**face** about 1,400 people and the total income amounted to $14,410.90. Of this **sum** $8,511.72 were expended upon the cemetery, including $1,500 the directory paid towards the Soldiers-Monument of the Catholic Veteran Association, leaving a **surplus** of $5,899.18.

This cemetery is rich in costly monuments, an indication that many of those who ended their life's pilgrimage here, have left their families in very comfortable circumstances. The majority of the older monuments are of marble, but those erected more recently are made of lasting granite, which can better resist the elements, than marble and softer stone.

The Soldiers monument, unveiled and consecrated on Decoration Day a **few** years ago, is a great ornament to the cemetery. The other monuments

Soldier's Monument in Rosehill.

deserving special mention are those of Joseph Haunschild, Marie New, Anton Schillo, John C. Roeder, Chr. Brick, Amelia C. Boyle, John Temple, Michael Sieben, Chas. Dominick Miville, John Zender, Anton Detmer, F. Scholer, Nicolas and Leo P. Leiendecker, Mich. Diversy, Henry Wischemeyer, John Herting, J. Schoenewald, A. Hagemann, A. Baier, John B. Busch, A. Zulfer, Anton Cremer, Bernard Müller, Catharine Hechinger, J. Arnold, Albert Wagner, the Pfeifer family, Marie Siedek, Peter Wagner, Felix Blatter, M. Coss mann, F. Mayer, Louise Hesing, etc.

Of these the last named monument in the south-eastern portion of the cemetery ranks first in the choice of the subject as well as in the artistic execution of the same. Certainly in no other are the characteristic virtues of the deceased expressed so well symbolically and perpetuated as in this granite statue of *St. Elizabeth*, erected to the memory of Mrs. Louise Hesing. It was indeed a happy thought to decorate the grave of this noble woman, who knew no greater joy than to do good and make happy the oppressed and needy, with an almost life-like representation of the saint, whom we are wont to look upon as the ideal of the purest charity.

The statue measures 7 feet 6 inches in height and represents the pious landgravine of Thuringia, distributing bread to the poor with her outstretched right hand. In the folds of her dress, which she holds with her left, are seen the roses, into which the victuals she was carrying to the poor of the City of Eisenach, changed at the moment when her husband, the landgrave Ludwig, forced open the basket in which she carried her charitable gifts from the castle. The model for this statue was executed by Mr. F. Engelsmann, a talented young German artist, and the statue itself, measuring with the base 9 feet 6 inches, was made at the steam granite works of Burkhardt and Son, No. 138 Kingsbury Street, Chicago. The monument is cut out of light-gray Westerley, (R. I.) granite, which, owing to its hardness and other desirable properties, is especially adapted to monuments. Upon the front of the base above the simple inscription: *Louise Hesing,* is seen a bronze-medallion of the deceased, also the work of Mr. Engelsmann.

The special merit of the statue lies in the mild and loving expression of the face, in which are plainly reflected nobility of soul and kindness of heart. It is scarcely necessary to say, that the figure bears also in every other part the mark of high artistic ability The grave of Mrs. Hesing is covered with a thick mass of blooming evergreen.

The lot of Marie New is ornamented with figures representing a mother and child, whilst the monument of Christian Brick is in the shape of a Christ-chapel. Upon the foundation supporting the monument on the grave of Amelia C. Boyle a female figure is represented resting upon a cross, symbolizing mourning. The monument of John Zender consists of a pyramid of rocks upon which stands Jesus with the Cross. Very expressive is the monument on the grave of F. Scholer. It represents a block of stone with cross and anchor, which latter is fastened with a rope cut out of the rock to the (stone) trunk of a tree rising in the middle. The tall marble monument of John Herting is crowned by the life-size figure of St. Boniface. Many other monuments could be mentioned if the space would permit, but it may here be mentioned, that besides the statue of St. Elizabeth *Mr. Burkhardt* has made many monuments for St. Boniface and other cemeteries, which are notable for their originality and artistic value and are not copies of models too frequently copied.

Among others furnished by him, the Wacker monument at Graceland is especially conspicuous.

We may conclude this article with the translation of two lines we have found upon a grave-stone in the old portion of St. Boniface:

" Thee, also, death will call away,
Thou, too, wilt in thy grave decay."

WUNDER'S CHURCH-YARD.
JEWISH CEMETERIES.

The greatest difficulties managers of burial places meet with, are encountered by German churches, who have established their own cemeteries. In the German mind the resting-places of the dead are inseparately connected with their religious life and church associations. Their cemeteries are consecrated spots, "church-yards," "fields of peace," "God's acres." They do not like to be buried outside of these, and therefore all German congregations aim to have their own burying ground. But they generally consist of working people, who hardly ever have much beyond their needs. It is therefore not an easy thing for them to accumulate enough wealth, wherewith to purchase a piece of ground sufficiently large to receive their dead during generations, and it is equally difficult for them to keep it in order, as that requires a constant outlay of money; neither can they ask for their lots any such sums as are paid in the larger cemeteries. The consequences are, that the graves have to be used over and over again and have to be largely left to themselves or to the care of the relatives of the interred.

Though the congregations who bury their dead in Wunder's cemetery are doing their very best to overcome these difficulties, the aforementioned evils are nevertheless sadly noticeable. There are portions of it, however, which are well kept and are in every way in keeping with the solemnity of the place. A decided step towards a thorough improvement of the cemetery is a recent resolution of the management, not to permit any more interments in single graves, but only in family lots. That, if anything, will insure a better state of things.

The cemetery is situated but a few feet south of Graceland and was consecrated in the beginning of the fifties. How many were buried there in the course or the last forty years, cannot be determined, owing to the repeated use of the same graves. The family lots are chiefly found in the front part of this German necropolis and as a rule show loving care. Upon many of them are seen fine monuments, some of which have artistic value. A very pleasing feature are the inscriptions upon these monuments, tomb-stones and even the plain wood crosses adorning the graves of the poorer of those sleeping there, which are mainly of a religious character. Some also tell a sad story, as the inscription on the obelisk just opposite the gate does, which runs in German: "Wanderer, stand still! Here rests in God a true husband and father, who had to lose his life in his calling as fireman," and in English: "John Streming, killed at a fire on South Water Street, June 8th, 1865, while on Duty."

On the more beautiful of the monuments the following names are inscribed: Charlotte Becker, John Janke, Family Fiedler, William Hallermann, C. Sprengel, A Drechsler, Ludwig Sommer, Friedrich Hoermann, Albert T. Haeberle, Amanda Hallermann, Conrad Oberg, F. Schramm, Heinrich Junker, Dora Lasman, Henry Schultz. Wm. Rohn, L. Hildenbeutel, John G. Dohl, and others.

Just on the other side of the fence, south of Wunder's Church Yard, is a Jewish cemetery, which presents a very pleasing appearance. Everything there is kept in the best of order. The signs above the gate show that several congregations bury their dead in these grounds. One sign reads: Chebra Gemilothe Chassadim U'bikor Cholim, and another: "Hebrew Benevolent Society," besides these also the "Bnai Sholem" congregation buries its dead in this place.

Graceland,

A. N. MARQUIS & CO.

The cemetery contains five acres of land. The family lots as well as most of the single graves are not only well-kept, but show tender care. The roads and paths also are well cared for by the attendant, a Swede named P. N. Neiglick, and he being a gardener, the place everywhere shows his skill and good taste. Mr. Neiglick is of the Christian faith, but attends to his duties in the Jewish burial place with as much reverence as a Jew could do. He receives no regular salary for his services, but contents himself with his income from the sale of flowers and plants for decorating purposes and from the care of graves.

In this cemetery about 2000 people are buried, of whom not a few were laid to rest here at the expense of Societies. There is no lack of handsome monuments. The inscriptions on some of them testify to the tendency on the part of many Jewish people to anglicise and corrupt their honest and generally very pretty German names, in such a degree that they hardly can be recognized in their new English dress.

Among the monuments which deserve to be specially mentioned there are those of: Morris Rosenfeld, Herman Seaman, Isaac Goldstein, Isaac Waitzel, Moses Ruhl, M. M. Spiegel, H. L. Marks, Henry Abrahams, Marcus Jampolis, David Adams, Heiman Solomon, Jacob Pieser, P. Goldstein, Shrimski, Samuel Goldmann, etc.

The cemetery was opened in the summer of 1854 and the body of Ida Kohn, who was buried there on August 6th of that year, was the first one laid to rest there.

Further south on Clark Street, at the southwest corner of Belmont Avenue, formerly was situated the cemetery of the *Anshe Mayrice* congregation. The same contained about four acres, and was laid out in 1856. But the congregation recently had another cemetery surveyed, of which it now has taken possession. It is located in Jefferson in the neighborhood of the Cook County Poor House, and contains 20 acres, five times the territory of the old one. The remains of those buried in the old grounds together with a number of the monuments have all been transferred to the new cemetery. The number of bodies that had been interred in the old grounds was 985. Here too, formerly a number of monuments were standing, which cost a great deal of money and at the same time furnishes further proof of the corruption of names. On one appeared the name of Falk Austrian, whilst along side of it stood an older tomb-stone for which the good German name of *Oesterreicher* had evidently been still considered good enough; the inscription there read: "*Malla, wife of Abraham Oesterreicher.*"

OAKWOODS CEMETERY.

This beautiful cemetery stands in the front rank, as one of the handsomest of Chicago's burial grounds. It is located south of 67th St. between Cottage Grove Ave. and the I. C. R. R. track. The distance from the business centre is about seven miles. It is reached by the "Hyde Park" cable trains, and by the I. C. and Pittsburgh & Ft. Wayne R. R's. It is also easily accessible by several convenient carriage drives. There are numerous dwellings in the immediate vicinity of this cemetery, nevertheless, Oakwoods is protected from future interference, and guaranteed absolute permanency by a special charter of the legislature.

In drawing the plan for the grounds, the Association was fortunate in securing the services of the late Mr. Adolph Strauch, Superintendent of Spring Grove Cemetery, at Cincinnati, who as a landscape gardener and Superintendent of cemeteries, probably had no equal. Before work was commenced in 1864, he visited and made a thorough examination of the land, and assured the Association that it was well adapted for the purpose it was designed for. Then, with a detailed survey, showing the surface elevation, he drafted the plan now presented to the public, designating the lowest land for artificial lakes, and the higher to be made still higher, and formed into beautiful mounds with the earth taken from the lakes.

The avenues are laid out in gentle curves and on an established grade. Perfect drainage of the surveyed portion is secured by judicious grading. The land is of a gravelly, sandy nature; the kind best suited for sepulture, and is covered by a good soil of considerable depth, ensuring a vigorous growth of grass, trees, shrubbery and flowers.

Like other cemeteries that can lay claim to landscape beauties, Oakwoods is devoid of fences and enclosures that often surround burial lots; it is arranged on the lawn system, by which the natural charm of the scenery is sustained. It is ornamented and kept like a park, at the same time being invested with all the sacredness and solemnity befitting a burial place for the dead.

Oakwoods comprises a territory of 184 acres, of which a little less than half is now in use. The first burial took place on May 20th, 1865. It is now the silent abode of the mortal remains of nearly 20,000 former inhabitants of this city. The cemetery company has recently erected a fine building at an expenditure of $10,000. It contains the office, store-room, etc. Also a magnificent entrance, consisting of a number of highly-polished granite shafts, arranged in the most presentable manner, forming a new departure in the architecture of cemetery gateways. The design for this really handsome gateway and entrance was furnished by Mr. Marcus A. Farwell, the popular President of the Association, and it does him great credit.

The charming residence of director H. H. Sheppard is situated near the main entrance. Close to this are the large green-houses, of which there are not less than ten; the dimensions of each being 100 ft. long and 20 ft. wide. They are under the supervision of the skilful head gardener, Alexander Reed. All varieties of rare flowers are cultivated here, and used in the ornamentation of the graves, and for other purposes. The company derives a handsome revenue from the sale of flowers and plants alone. A separate office is used, and a force of clerks employed, to supply the demands of patrons.

The water-works are near to this, which supply about 5 miles of water pipes. The water works system is entirely independent of any outside appliance. There are five artificial lakes of considerable size, the banks of which are sloping lawns to the waters edge.

In Oakwoods there are many costly monuments and mausoleums, and a spacious vault connected with a chapel building. The vault has a capacity for holding 500 bodies, and is built in the latest and most approved style.

Gateway to Oakwoods Cemetery.

Upon entering, the first conspicuous monument that meets the eye is that of Conrad Seipp, a granite obelisk with urn attached. The following is a partial list of the more costly monuments, to be found in this cemetery Those of Wm. H. Newman, Jos. E. C. Zeller, Wm. H. Harper, Mead Mason, John N. Gage, Van Bokellen, Lena Robinson, S. M. T. Turner, Israel Holmes, Sam. R. Noe, Alphonso Goodrich, Wm. S. Hancock, F. K. Dunn, Frank Drake, Cyrus E. Cole, Harry W Phillips, Gabriel Steiger, L. G. Gall, Henry Hoyt, Dan'l Goodman, Henry A. Spence, Frank Van Houtin, David Burcky, Nellie W. Ullmann, Giesbert Pottgieser, F Kublank, Louise Lehrkamp, F. Sorgenfrei, George Kress, August Keller, J Werkmeister, E T Wadlow, C. Gieliske, C. F. Kauffert, August Geilfuss, A. J. W. Jahncke, Emma W. Jacob, Paul Kleiner, Wm. Hickling, Paul Cornell, Chas. Stein, Ben Carver, Burton C. Cook, Christian Schmidt, Chas. Tessmann, Peter Abt, Henry Apple, Henry G. Oehmich, John H. McAvoy, Robert Cunningham, Angus, James Campbell, H. H. Cooley, Williams, W. H. Schimpfermann, H. Guth, B. Artz, Conrad Stuckart and Catharine Friesleben. The monument of Cale Cramer, who lost his life July 27, 1887, in a collision near York, Ind., consists of a shattered locomotive of stone. The soldiers' monument was erected by one of the directors of the Chicago Soldiers' Home. The statue represents a private soldier with his rifle, and is finished in stone; the pedestal consists of marble. In the foreground there are four cannons guarding the graves of about 70 veterans.

The remains of over 5,000 Confederate soldiers, who died at Camp Douglas, (a war-prison, situated on Cottage Grove Avenue during the late war), are interred here in a thicket of elms. The local society of confederate soldiers, have in contemplation the erection of a suitable monument to the memory of their departed comrades. Jeff. Davis himself, in his lifetime, evinced great interest in the erection of this memorial. Oakwoods contains also two small Jewish cemeteries of the congregations of Beth Hamedrash, and Ohoveh Shemil, respectively one acre and one half acre in dimensions.

That this cemetery can never be diverted from its present use and purpose is fully guaranteed in the following section of the charter: "And no road, street, alley or thoroughfare shall be laid out or opened through their said grounds, or any part thereof, without the consent of the directors; nor shall any corporation now existing, or hereafter created, be authorized to take, hold or possess any portion of said cemetery by condemnation, without such consent." Oakwoods is one of the very few cemeteries in Cook County that is organized under a special charter granted by the Legislature, which protects it from interference, and guarantees its absolute permanency. No cemetery organized since the adoption of the present State Constitution, which took effect in 1870, has or can obtain a special charter. Under the present laws all new cemeteries are liable to be ruined by common roads, streets and railroads being forced through them. They have no protection like those organized under the old special charters. This cemetery has every security that the State of Illinois, through its Legislature, can confer. Oakwoods Cemetery is indeed a rural cemetery, and the Original Rural Cemetery of Chicago, ornamented and kept like a highly cultivated park, while at the same time it is invested with all the sacredness pertaining to a burial place for the dead. The Association makes the improvements, grades the lots, excavates the lakes, and plants ornamental trees. The prices of lots vary from fifty cents to one dollar per square foot, according to location. The price at present for a single grave for an adult is ten dollars; for children, six to eight dollars.

The funeral trains by the Illinois Central Railroad leaving the city at 2 and 3 P. M. go to the cemetery gate. The Pittsburgh & Fort Wayne Railroad suburban trains also stop at Cottage Grove Avenue, near the south-west corner of the grounds. There are good carriage roads from the City through Washington Park and Cottage Grove Avenue; also by 63rd, South Park Avenue and 67th Street.

The officers of the company are: Marcus A. Farwell, President; James McKindley, Vice President; W. C. D. Grannis, Treasurer; George M. Bogue, Secretary, and J. H. Shepard, Superintendent.
6

ST. MARIA. — MT. GREENWOOD.

Of the four cemeteries situated beyond the southwestern limits of the City: St. Maria, Mt. Greenwood, Mt. Olivet and Mt. Hope, the first named lies nearest to the City and is the one where the funeral trains of the Grand Trunk Railroad coming from the city make their first stop.

ST. MARIA CEMETERY

is a German Catholic burying ground, which was consecrated on May 13, 1888, by Archbishop Feehan in the presence of a large concourse of people. Its northern boundary line is formed by Eighty-seventh street; the cemetery contains one hundred and two acres of ground, which lie on the western slope of Washington heights at an elevation of fifty-five feet above the level of Lake Michigan and of from sixteen to twenty feet above the level of the surrounding prairie-land.

The German Catholics of the South and Southwest Sides have long felt the need of a burying ground somewhere near the southern limits of Chicago, where those of their people, who died in the Catholic faith, could find a final resting place, but not until the year 1887 had nearly passed was there an earnest effort made in this direction. Then it was that through the generosity of Heinrich Wischemeyer and his wife Maria, the Association which has also control and the management of St. Boniface, the German Catholic cemetery on the North Side, was presented with sixty acres of the land which now forms St. Maria Cemetery, under the condition that the profits derived from the sale of lots and single graves be turned over to the Orphan Asylum at Roschill, which together with the two cemeteries is managed by a directory, chosen from the different German Catholic congregations of Chicago. After the sixty acres donated by Mr. and Mrs. Wischemeyer had been laid out and embellished, forty-two acres more of adjoining land was purchased at a very low figure.

Opposite the entrance gate on Eighty-seventh Street the management has erected a pretty depot-building in Swiss cottage-style. When the grounds passed into the possession of the association, the entire area showed neither tree nor shrub; to-day more than four thousand shade-trees of healthy growth are planted along the winding drives and foot-paths and scattered in picturesque groups all over the place, which at no distant day will equal any of the older cemeteries in point of landscape and general arrangement. The modern lawn-system has found favor here from the start and when the drives were mapped out, they were so arranged as to form a connecting system of carriage roads throughout the grounds. The different links of this chain of driveways have been given names such as: St. Anthony, St. Henry, St. Peter, St. Francis, St. Paul, St. George, St. Augustin, St. Martin, St. Ferdinand, St. Aloysius Avenue. At a central point where all the roads converge, a monument has been erected to the memory of Mr. and Mrs. Wischemeyer. It is hewn out of marble and is the gift of the Cemetery Association, who desired to express, in this manner its gratitude for the liberal donation of land by the honored couple. Not far from this monument, the receiving vault, a massive and spacious structure, arrests the attention of the visitor. It has room for four hundred coffins and is covered by a blue slate roof, beneath which two circular colored glass-windows admit the light of day to the interior. From here St. John's Avenue leads to the highest point of the cemetery, where we also find the dwelling of the sexton, who from his abode can overlook the entire territory under his immediate control.

At the suggestion of Rev. Peter Fischer, of St. Anthony's Church, who was the first president of the board of management, a novelty has been introduced in this cemetery, the like of which probably will not be met with in any other Catholic Cemetery. One of the choicest portions of the grounds, section A, has been set aside for the burial of families of mixed religion, so that the protestant wife of a catholic husband laid to rest here can be interred after her death by the side of her spouse and vice-versa.

Besides the Wischemeyer Memorial, there are several more very handsome monuments in this "God's Field," of which may be mentioned those of Michael Reidl of Englewood, Anton Tennie, August Bauer, Johann Ferber, Isabella Vaesgen (of Blue Island), John Wessendorf (Washington Heights), Theresa Gottsellig, Peter Thomas, etc. In wandering over that sacred ground and gazing upon the monuments soaring high in panegyric of the wealthy dead and upon the humble tombstones of those less favored when pilgrims of this world, now made equal though by the impartial hand of Death, we feel the belief grow within us, that there are sermons indeed which we may gather from Stones, and we also are fully convinced from what we see here, there and everywhere, that this German "Friedhof" will at some day near at hand, be not only one of the most interesting, but also one of the largest German Catholic cemeteries of this country.

MOUNT GREENWOOD CEMETERY.

This well known and beautiful cemetery is found three and a half miles south of St. Maria's on the Grand Trunk Railroad. It was opened to the public in 1879, and is situated upon the crest of Washington Heights and in the midst of a rolling country well covered with timber trees. Mt. Greenwood occupies the highest point of the chain of hills, which here rise to an elevation of seventy feet above the level of Lake Michigan. It contains eighty acres of land, of which no more than eighteen or twenty are used for purposes of sepulture. Here too the lawn-system is in full operation and was adopted in the beginning, so that Mt. Greenwood comes under the head of Park Cemeteries. The winding, serpentine drives are mostly macadamized and kept in excellent repair. The first body was buried here April 28, 1880, and since then more than three thousand people, who had ended life's pilgrimage, were interred under the mighty oaks that stand sentinel within the inclosures of Mt. Greenwood. Much importance is placed here on the propagation of plants for ornamenting graves and lawns and the lovely and tasteful beds of flowers that in summer meet the eye everywhere, give sufficient evidence of the earnest aim of the management, to make this Burial Park another point of interest for friends and strangers, for in point of decoration it will take rank with many ornate parks and gardens.

The entrance is situated on 111th Street, east of the railroad station, and is flanked on the righthand side by the cemetery office, constructed nearly altogether out of the limbs and bark of trees, and over all climbing plants have woven an emerald awning. The cultivation of plants and flowers is carried on within three roomy green-houses which have a length of one hundred feet each. The public vault, situated in close proximity to the plant houses, has a capacity for holding five hundred coffins; there are many elegant and costly monuments, of which a few only may be mentioned. The one most prominent and conspicuous among them is the obelisk of the dead philantropist, Karl Uhlich; it towers into the air to a height of thirty-three feet and is crowned by a female figure, symbolizing Hope. The wife of Uhlich, four of their children, and Henry Klein, an old and trusted friend of the Uhlich family, are all buried in the shadow of the obelisk. Of the other monuments, those of Herman Vanderbelt, Mary Adelheid Brockway, Wm. Morgan, (Blue Island), N. B. Rexford, Benjamin Kayler (the original owner of the land), the "Elks," Edgar Johnson Goodspeed, Walter Pride Cottle, etc. have great artistic merit.

MT. OLIVET.

This Catholic cemetery is situated directly opposite the entrance to Mt. Greenwood, south of One hundreth and eleventh street, from where it extends as far as One hundred and fifteenth street. Like Mt. Greenwood and Mt. Hope it is located on high and hilly ground and therefore even in the wettest season the ground remains dry and is therefore all the more suitable for the purpose it is intended for. This cemetery with its abundance of stately oaks has more the resemblance of a sylvan grove than of a city of the dead. It contains eighty acres, of which about half are in use. The dedication of this beautiful "Gods' Acre" took place June 28th, 1885, and since that time over 4000 bodies have been laid to rest there.

Mt. Olivet is under the same management as Calvary Cemetery. The land was purchased in September, 1884, from the late Judge Beckwith, and June 17th, of the following year the first burial took place there. The general appearance of Mt. Olivet gives evidence of the fact, that an earnest and successful effort is made to keep the grounds in good trim, and to permit nothing which might prove an eyesore or challenge unfavorable criticism.

Among the monuments seen here and there the one erected by the Irish Nationalists is the most conspicuous, it is a granite obelisk thirteen feet high. Other memorials worthy of mention are those of Abraham Raimburg, James Shay, John Flannigan, Carl Miller, Martin Hogan, William Pauly, P. C. McDonald, etc.

This cemetery is provided with a water-windmill and other facilities for assisting nature in its work of beautifying this forest-like burial ground, by which the latter admirably succeeds in assuming the character of a cheerful park and in losing more and more those features that gave to it at first a gloomy and dismal appearance.

The establishment of Mt. Olivet has proven a great convenience for the Catholics residing in the extreme southern parts of our city, who in former times were compelled to travel from 15 to 20 miles each way when accompanying a deceased relative or friend way out north to Calvary Cemetery.

It is the intention of the management to build a large receiving-vault at Mt. Olivet in the near future, and from what we have observed in Calvary, the twin-brother of Mt. Olivet, the latter will certainly in due time be still more embellished and improved and then it will be one of the most attractive park-cemeteries of our city.

Rosehill.—Monument of Prof. Cumming Cherry.

MOUNT HOPE.

This beautiful Park Cemetery is situated on that ridge of wooded hills, southwest of the city, commonly known as Washington Heights, and directly west of, and adjoining Morgan Park. This location was decided upon after a careful survey of all the available property for such purposes, in Cook County, south and west of the city. It is emphatically the best selection that could have been made. It consists of three hundred acres in a compact body. The association has a capital of $600,000.00, and for five years has had a large force of men working under the direction of the best obtainable engineers and landscape gardeners, in bringing this immense property to a state of perfection.

No money has been spared in making this cemetery, what its founders intend it shall be—the model cemetery of the country. They have erected a fine stone chapel, depot, waiting rooms and office, costing about $20,000. The public vault is the most complete of any in the west, and contains one hundred and sixty separate iron compartments. The splendid growth of native oaks, which cover the hills, has been interplanted by an immense number of all varieties of ornamental trees and shrubs. The finely paved roads that traverse the grounds in all directions, and wind among the hills, produce a most pleasing and finished effect. The lake, the flowers, the turf; all combine to make it an ornamental park, in the truest sense of the word. An abundant supply of pure water for all purposes is furnished from an artesian well. Steam pumping works distribute this over the cemetery, through a system of iron pipes. Although it lies 100 feet above the level of Lake Michigan and the soil is of the most suitable character for cemetery purposes—yet that there might be no possible doubt as to its freedom from water —these natural advantages have been supplemented by an elaborate system of surface and under drainage. The beauty of the cemetery is marvelous. No pen picture can do it justice. It must be seen to be appreciated.

When this cemetery was laid out and beautified, Chicago had another park added to those which have already made her world-famous. But it differs from the pleasure grounds in which the toiling thousands take their rest every Sunday in the summer; for in the new garden where art and nature vie with each other in creating a scene of loveliness, every day will be a Sabbath and the beauty will be consecrated not to the living but to the dead.

The enterprise which has selected these grounds on Washington Heights —aimed to give to a great city another park cemetery, which is worthy of its greatness and represents in its highest developement the advanced taste which the present century has brought to bear upon the resting place of the dead. Not only is the civilization of a people expressed in the avenues of palatial homes and in the imposing edifices of commerce, but also in the condition of their places of sepulture. The tomb is to the future the witness of the present; it carries to posterity the records of a generation's ideals, whether they be high or low, debased or noble. In the monuments of the antique world we read the history of her tyranny, of her superstition, of her moments of enfranchisement and of her years of darkness; and the enlightenment of this age—the enlightenment of widespread education, charity and freedom—will not be less truly mirrored in the cemeteries which we establish and adorn and which we leave for the edification of posterity. It would be strange if the progress of knowledge, which has done so much for the material comforts of life and the beautifying of homes, did not also rob death of some of its distressing associations and make the last of all homes more endurable to man's contem-

plation. Science has not been idle in this respect. Seconded by the growing
sense of human refinement, she has in the last few years removed the dis-
agreeable features remaining from the practices of the past, and has invested
places of interment with suggestions of beauty that are pleasing to the
senses and elevating to the soul. The old style of graveyard, with its rectan-
gular form, its huddled hillocks which seem to cry out against the parsimony
of earth in not affording ample resting place to her children, and in its dis-
cordant and often distasteful and memorial symbols, is happily now a thing of
the past, and one that can never be recalled. Hereafter the parks in which
the living take their pleasure shall not be more enchanting than those where
peace guards the pillow of rest. It must be said that Chicago is not first
among the cities in the idea of an ornamental cemetery, though she is easily
first in her parks and boulevards and her avenues of architectural splendor.

The promoters of park cemeteries have to fight some lingering prejudices
in the minds of people who look with apprehension upon any departure from
custom; but these prejudices disappear when it is made plain that the new
departure is in the interest both of economy and of estheticism. How much
better is it, for instance, that the money spent upon stone copings and iron
railings (barriers that imply the idea that some sort of outrage might be possible) were devoted instead to raising a monument of enduring qualities and
of truly artistic design. Experience has shown that railings and copings in-
variably fall into disorder through exposure to the severe temperature, and
the result is that every old fashioned cemetery has upon its hands constantly
accumulating heaps of worthless stone and metal. Under the park plan, on
the contrary, large and roomy lots may be utilized, where, instead of incum-
brances in the shape of trivialities, one imposing shaft will serve as a family
monument, and where the sloping, grassy borders will give an effect im-
measurably more pleasing than that of forbidding hedges or of iron fences.

"The grave," says Washington Irving, "should be surrounded with
everything that may insure tenderness and veneration. Can this be done by
having burial lots enclosed with stone posts, iron bars and chains, the sight of
which is repulsive in the extreme, as it conveys the idea of rudeness and con-
finement?"

To everyone who is engaged in the busy struggle of existence it is now
consoling to know that his last resting place shall be made amidst scenes that
will charm rather than distress the beholder, and that will induce the visitor
to linger and feel half-loth to return to the busy haunts of men. The idea is
at once so tender and universal that it is not surprising that America's most
Horatian poet—William Cullen Bryant—should have given it the most exquisite expression

> I know, I know I should not see
>   The season's glorious show;
> Nor would its brightness shine for me
>   Nor its wild music flow;
> But if around my place of sleep
> The friends I love should come to weep,
>   They might not haste to go.
> Soft airs and song and light and bloom
> Should keep them lingering by my tomb.
> These to their softened hearts should bear
>   The thoughts of what has been,
> And speak of one who cannot share
>   The gladness of the scene.
> Whose part in all the pomp that fills
> The circuit of the summer hills
>   Is—that his grave is green.
> And deeply would their hearts rejoice
> To hear again his living voice.

Entrance to Forest Home.

FOREST HOME.

This cemetery is situated between West Madison and West Twelfth Sts., about four and one half miles west of the present City Limits, and embraces the most beautiful part of the once celebrated Haase's Park, comprising nearly one hundred acres of land. These grounds have gained a wide reputation for the beauty of their natural scenery; in fact their equal in that respect can not be found around Chicago. No spot could be more advantageously situated than the location of Forest Home, it being fifty-six feet above the level of Lake Michigan and the crown of the water-shed between the Atlantic and the Gulf. The water running from the roof of a house on the grounds on one side finds the St. Lawrence, while the drops that fall on the opposite side go to the Mississippi.

Comparatively few people in Chicago know what beautiful glimpses of Nature in her restful moods lie within easy reach of the city. The wheelmen are finding some of them, and every Sunday numbers of bicycles may be seen on the way west to the woods that border the Desplaines river. Artists too have learned of these spots, and views on the Desplaines are now to be seen at our art expositions both in oil and water colors. Years before the white man had come into this Western country the Indians had perceived the beauties of the natural park that borders the river between Harrison and Twelfth Streets, and had consecrated it to burials, and to-day there still remains undisturbed an Indian mound—the final record of a departed race. The Indian always selected for his camp and his burial Nature's choicest spots, and civilization has, in this place at least, confirmed his judgment and renewed the consecration—the limits of the Indian park now marking the boundaries of the most beautiful cemetery about Chicago. The prodigality of Nature in this beautiful spot seems to have inspired the management of the Forest Home Cemetery with a love of the beautiful. All improvements must be made on one general plan, and it is the aim to add to the natural beauties instead of dispelling them. "How appalling," says an eminent writer upon this subject, "are the acres of square plats and stone and iron inclosures that thrust the notion of property into your face at every turn, and at once break up the expression of the landscape and the thought that becomes the resting place of the dead." A glance at either of the views in Forest Home shows that in this resting place no such feeling comes to friend or stranger—Nature's beauties are unbroken. The visitor feels that his sympathy is not shut out by iron or stone, but that here private sorrow is lifted into universal fellowship. The "lawn system" adopted by the management is the system forshadowed in the article quoted from.

Notwithstanding its natural wildness and rural beauty, it is the most accessible of Chicago cemeteries. The Wisconsin Central and the electric cars on Madison Street land passengers almost at the gates of Forest Home. It is also connected with the city by well-kept roads on Madison and Twenty-second Sts. and Riverside Boulevard. A natural elevation in one part of the grounds has been taken advantage of by the management to erect a new vault for temporary purposes. It has an iron and glass roof just even with the surface of the ground, and runs back into the mound, leaving only the front in view, which opens upon a roadway extending along the face of the mound. A continuation of this elevation gives an opportunity for those preferring this manner of sepulture, to build and own private vaults, which can be entered from the drive.

Among the names of those who have secured resting places for their dead there are many of the prominent residents of our city and western suburbs. Handsome monuments mark the grave of Philander Smith, for many years a leading citizen of Oak Park; similar memorials adorn the beautiful lots of Edward G. Uihlein, a resident of Chicago, of H. W. Austin, and of C. H. Robinson, and of S. E. Hurlbut, Joseph Kettlestrings and Reuben Whaples, who were the first settlers of Oak Park, are buried here; and lots belonging to Clarence Cross, S. E. Hurlbut, George Eckart, E. H. Pitkin, J. H. Hurlbut and many others are pointed out.

Forest Home is the only one of Chicago's cemeteries at which the lawn system governed exclusively from the beginning; hence the uniform park like appearance of the grounds so much admired by all visitors. Under this system no coping or other means of marking the boundaries of lots can be used, except corner stones, and these must not rise more than six inches above the surface, thus making it easy to keep the lawns uniform. The Cemetery Company furnishes the corner stones with the name of the owner cut upon them free of charge. Aside from this, those purchasing lots in Forest Home under this system are exempt from all charges or assessments for keeping their lots in good order. One of the most commendable features of this cemetery is the "Perpetual Care Fund" established by the company a few years ago. This fund is created and continually augmented by semi-annual payments of ten per cent of the receipts from sale of lots by the Cemetery Company, and is entirely under the control and for the benefit of lot owners, ensuring them against any neglect of the grounds at any time hereafter. Of the roads leading to this cemetery, Madison Street, Riverside Boulevard and Twenty-second Street, should be preferred. Parties desiring to go by rail can take the Wisconsin Central main line to Forest Home Station, which is only a few blocks from the cemetery, or take the Electric Line from the terminus of West Madison Street cable car line to Forest Home.

As it was found desirable, that there be reserved, out of the gross income of this company, a fund to be used for the purpose of keeping in order, embellishing and improving the cemetery, at a time when the income from the sale of lots can no longer be used for that purpose by the Board of Directors, it was resolved, that there be created a fund, to be called the Forest Home Improvement Fund; which fund shall be under the sole and exclusive management and control of a BOARD OF TRUSTEES to be called the Trustees of the Forest Home Improvement Fund. The fund in question shall be created in the following manner: The Board of Directors shall retain out of the gross proceeds of the sale of lots, a sum equal to ten per centum, and pay the same over to said Board of Trustees. · The payments so to be made by the Board of Directors, shall cease, when the said fund reaches the sum of Twenty-five Thousand ($25,000) Dollars, and the performance of this undertaking on the part of the Forest Home Cemetery Company may be enforced at any time by a proper proceeding in equity, to be instituted in the names of the members of the Board of Trustees.

Scene In Forest Home.

WALDHEIM CEMETERY.

Situated in the town of Harlem, on the Desplaines River, and about nine miles from the city, is a German cemetery of exceptional beauty in its general aspect as well as in the tasteful and pleasing manner in which the various sections of the grounds have been laid out and changed into so many bright and cheerful garden spots   Like most of the other large cemeteries, Waldheim is open to all, and makes no distinction between the believer or unbeliever, between Christian, Jew or Heathen.   The park-like grounds contain 80 acres of well drained land, about half of which is still covered with a dense wood of healthy oak trees, whose days however are numbered.   During the last five or six years, improvements of a costly and quite an extensive character have been carried on here and wherever one casts his glance, he will see undoubted proofs of the earnest desire on the part the management, to leave nothing undone, that might tend to give greater perfection to the general system and create a source of gratification for the lot owners and visitors as well.   The remarkable success achieved by the management in this direction is due in a great measure to the untiring efforts of Mr. John Bähler, the secretary of the association, who devotes a great deal of his time to the active supervision of all matters concerning the cemetery, and to the good work done by Mr. George Schrade, the able superintendent.   The management succeeded in inducing the Wisconsin Central Railroad to extend their tracks to the northeast corner of the enclosure on Desplaines Avenue, whereby it was made possible to bring the funeral trains within a few steps of the main entrance; besides these means of transportation the Electric Street Railway, which connects with the cable trains on Madison Street at West Fortieth Street, runs its cars up Desplaines Avenue to the imposing, castle like cemetery gate.   The latter contains a spacious chapel on the right hand side and the business office of the superintendent on the left.   From the books in this office can be ascertained, that the first interment took place on May 7, 1873, and that the bodies laid to rest there since, number more than 16,000.

Immediately after passing through the gateway and passing along the main drive leading therefrom, we find ourselves in the midst of a large open meadow, tastefully planted with trees and shrubs and further embellished by two small artificial lakes, their mirror-like surface reflecting the azure of the sky and the swiftly fleeing clouds.   On each side of the well kept drives and paths stretches of fresh green turf meet the eye, relieved by the darker clumps of shrubs, by flowers and trees and by the scattered monuments, which indicate the purposes of the place.

Here a spacious burial-lot can be obtained at a moderate sum by every household, that shall remain an heirloom forever sacred and inviolate.   Kindred of several generations can repose together, and they may adorn their burial place with such works of art, as affection shall dictate.   And not only single families, but kindred and affiliated branches and societies may choose their resting places side by side, the ties of friendship and consanguinity, strong in life, not wholly sundered in death.   Waldheim, the German for Forest Home, does not blind us to the fact of our mortality—it cannot and should not—but it brings the fact before us in the least forbidding form and in such connections, that, while we are subdued and solemnized, we are also sustained and cheered.   So that, while we stand and look upon the grave, all manner of pleasant images rise before us.   Waldheim is not a door leading into darkness, but the gate of glory, where friends come to say their last farewells.   It is one of those cemeteries, happily becoming more and more numerous, where in a conspicuous way, *gardenesque* adornment is especially noticeable, far different from many of the old burying grounds, so forlorn and hideous, that the school-boy hurries past them in affright and both young and old shudder at the thought of being finally deposited there.   It is near enough to the city, as to be easy of access at all seasons of the year and yet not so nigh, as to sacrifice aught of its sacredness and privacy, or that it will ever be liable to encroachment by the demands of commerce or population.

Waldheim, while not possessing the frigid stateliness of a public park, or the elaborate decorations and high finish of a suburban country-seat, is truly a secluded, cultivated scene, with **no** air of presumption or unfitting display and awakening no thoughts **except** those of security, repose, affectionate remembrance, cheerful hope, in **fine, the** grounds wear an expression of solemnity and subdued beauty

In reference to the portion yet covered with **forest oaks, it is proposed to** thin them out from year to year, removing first **the oldest and those showing** signs of decay, then the tall and meagre and finally **all except those standing** near the avenues or in certain spaces intended for driveways. **It is no longer** permitted to surround burial lots with unsightly **iron palisades or stone enclos**ures, because the management is following the **example set down by other** progressive cemetery-gardeners, and long ago **became determined to avail** itself of the advantages offered by the lawn system.

The living owners of burial lots and graves seem to **take** great pride in the tasteful embellishment of those spots so dear to them, **and they** thereby greatly assist the cemetery management in their praiseworthy **efforts, to** press upon every thing within the enclosure the stamp of harmony and attractiveness. The number of neglected or forgotten graves is insignificantly **small.** Throughout the cemetery parterres of sweet scented flowers, picturesque trees and clumps of evergreens are scattered in the most appropriate spots. The beau**ties** of the place, indeed, appear to be fully appreciated, for the garden, as **we** may **not** inappropriately call the grounds, are fairly filled with **persons, not** only **on** Sundays, but on every week day during the summer **months,** evidently enjoying the quiet, the pure air and the charming landscape.

Quite a number of German Societies are the owners of lots here, upon which some of them, the Druids and Odd Fellows for instance, have erected splendid monuments of great artistic merit. Besides these there are the German Society, German Altenheim, German Hospital, Aurora Turnverein, Turnverein "Vorwaerts," Schleswig-Holstein Benevolent Society, Lodges from the Orders of Harugari and Sons of Hermann, Herder Lodge from the Order of Free Masons, Order of Red Men, Social Workingmens' Society of the West Side, etc. As is well known, the friends of the executed anarchists were permitted by the Waldheim Association to lay the bodies of their so called "Martyrs" to rest in this cemetery. They were buried near the southern driveway in a very choice section of the grounds, where their common grave is crowned by a marble head stone, and covered with beds of flowers. **The burial** lot contains 1,500 square feet and is enclosed by an iron chain; **in the near** future a large monument with allegorical figures is to take **the place of the** present low head stone. **In** the southwestern **corner** of the **cemetery a Jewish** congregation buries its **dead.**

Upon the **monuments that are above** mediocrity **and show** good taste, as well as the skill of the sculptor, **the** following names are inscribed: Troost Bros., Arno Voss, Werner Clussmann, U. Seyfried, Wilhelmine Hellwig, Geo. Jansen, Louise **and** Wilhelm Schroeder, Jacques Fröhlich, Mathias Schulz, H. Wiemann, John **B.** Müller, N. Righeimer, Anton Schuerle, Friedrich Maas, Joseph Fischer, **M.** Gottfried, John L. Hörber, E. R. Lott, John Kummer, B. L. Roos, Johanna Hohner, G. Tarnow, J. Hanke, Peter Koehler, Minna Maurer, — Bodenschatz, Margarethe Underberg, John H. Schmidt, Auguste Zöllner, John Trogg, A. Delp, Moritz Langeloth, John Bühler, etc.

It remains yet to be mentioned that Waldheim also contains a spacious receiving vault built after the most approved fashion and located on the main driveway.

The directors of Waldheim Cemetery are: John Buehler, **Jos.** Fischer, C. F. Geist, Wm. Feindt, Phil. Maas, Jacob Heissler, John Lingenberg, **T. J.** Lefens, G. Schweinfurth, John M. Faulhaber, Dr. Theo. Wild, Theo. Guenther, H. N. Lafrentz and W. C. Seipp. The following are the officers: Phil. Maas, president; Jacob Heissler, vice-president; J. M. Faulhaber, treasurer; John Buehler, secretary; G. Schrade, superintendent.

Entrance to Waldheim Cemetery.

EIGHT SMALL JEWISH CEMETERIES

are established on both sides of the road leading from Forest Home to River-side, and about one mile distant from the latter cemetery. On the signs that overhang the entrance-gates, the names of the congregations and societies who own these burying places are painted as follows: "Austrian-Hungarian Benev-olent Society;" "Anshe Suwalk, Chicago;" "Chewre Anshe Emes;" "Moses Montefiore;" "Ohavo Amuno;" "B'nai Abraham." "Improved Order of Free Sons;" "Free Sons of Israel." The cemetery of the last named Order, which is composed of ten Chicago lodges, is the largest and by far the handsomest of them all; it is evident from the general appearance of the grounds that they were laid out and embellished with excellent taste. This cemetery is situated between the roadway and the Desplaines river, the shores of which at that point are beautifully ornamented with stately trees, whose heavy green foliage forms a very effective background to these villages of the dead. The opening of the cemetery owned by the "Free Sons of Israel" took place in 1876, and since then more than a hundred bodies were laid to rest there. The directors have expended over $10,000 for improvements, and they have spared no efforts to keep pace with the progress made elsewhere in cemetery-work and to provide these grounds with all the cheerful and yet solemn aspects which we look for in a model cemetery. The original cost of the five acres of land was $1200, and in the beginning, lots 12 x 16 feet were sold to members at $10 each. To-day the value of lots of the same size has advanced to $50. The cemetery is open not only to members of the Order and the poor it assists and buries, but also to Jews who do not belong to the organization.

The burial ground of the "Improved Free Sons of Israel," directly opposite the cemetery of the "Free Sons" without the prefix "Improved" has been sold, as the Order went out of existence; seemingly it did not prove an "Improve-ment" on the old Order of Free Sons.

CONCORDIA CEMETERY

is situated in the town of Harlem on the Desplaines river, about nine miles
west from the City Hall. The main entrance is on Madison Street, directly
west of the German Old People's Home. This is a German Lutheran Cemetery containing 60 acres of well drained land and is under the management
of seven Lutheran Congregations. The grounds everywhere show scrupulous
care and bear evidence that the management is liberal in its expenditures for
necessary improvements. More than half of the entire territory, of which 16
acres are situated south of the Minnesota & Northwestern railroad tracks, has
been laid out and devoted to purposes of interment. According to an established rule enclosures of any kind are not permitted around burial lots and
another very wise rule obligates the cemetery-superintendent to keep the
walks and drives clean and in good condition, to allow no weeds to disfigure
lawns or graves, to keep the grass low and the flowers on the little mounds
well watered during dry seasons.

The total number of bodies buried in Concordia reaches nearly 16,000, of
which about half are slumbering in single graves. The cemetery was dedicated and opened in 1872, but not until the association was incorporated as a
stock company in 1884, was there more than ordinary importance placed
upon beautifying and embellishing the grounds. Among the later improvements a massive and ornamental entrance gate and public vault with space
for 400 coffins were the most significant and necessitated an outlay of about
$15,000. The building forming the entrance gate contains the office of the
superintendent, a waiting room and storage cellars. The bell-tower crowning this structure has a height of 55 feet and is covered with copper and slate.
Besides the improvements mentioned the windmill-pump erected a few years
ago also plays an important part among the resources of this model grave-
yard, which is reached by taking the cable and electric cars on Madison Street,
or the trains of the Wisconsin Central Railroad.

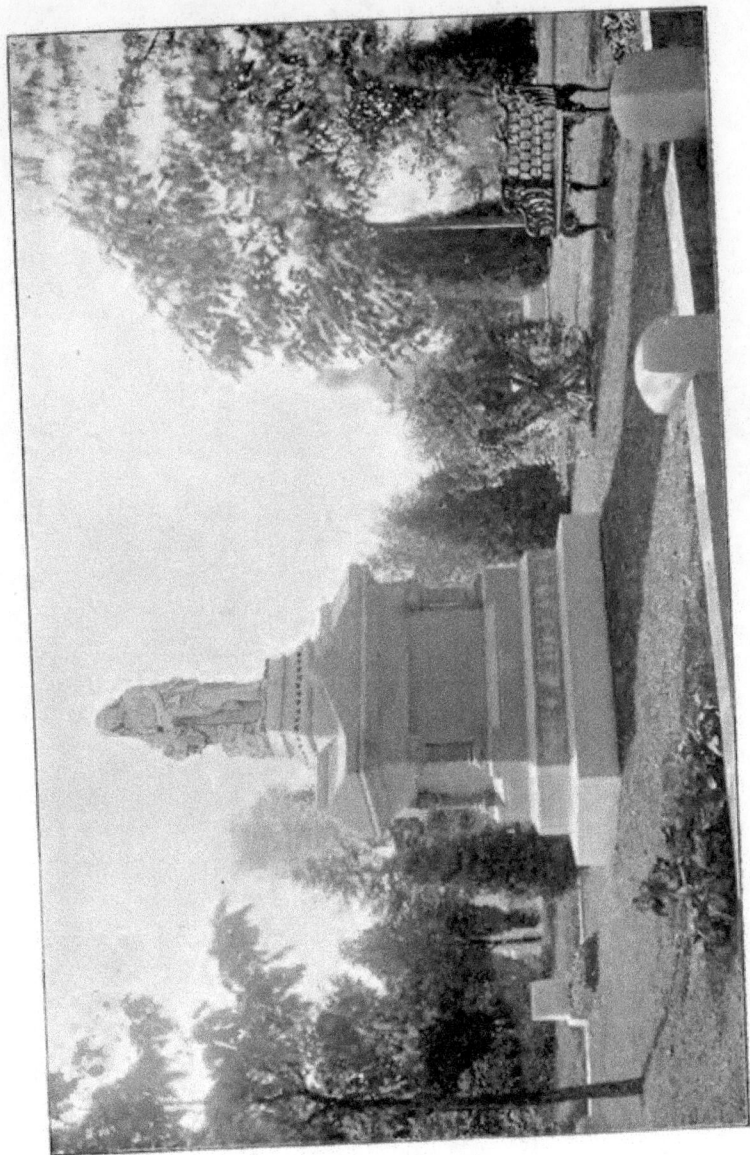

Waldheim.—Monument of John Buehler.

MOUNT OLIVE.

This charming cemetery is situated near the County Institutions at Dunning, in the Town of Jefferson, on the Chicago, Milwaukee & St. Paul R. R. It can justly lay claim to the designation charming, for it unites in a very high degree the beauties of a park garden with the repose and solemnity of a city of the dead. Within the enclosures of this God's Acre there are 52½ acres of high and dry land, laid out in blocks and lots and single graves, planted with stately trees, flowering shrubs and children of the garden flora, the emblems of love, faith and charity.

Although Mount Olive is one of the youngest among Chicago's park-cemeteries, it has nevertheless gained quite an enviable reputation for itself as a burying ground, combining all the elements and advantages, that make up a model cemetery.

It was turned over to public use in August, 1886, and is now the last resting place of over 7,000 former inhabitants of Chicago. The lawn system was adopted from the first and what has been done under this system so far, shows excellent taste and a thorough knowledge of landscape gardening. Enchanting views are obtained at different points about the grounds; quite a peculiar feature of this "Yard of Peace" are a number of well developed crab apple trees, which, when laden with their ripe, golden fruit in Autumn, lend a singular beauty to the picturesque landscape all around. Adjoining these fruit trees a small grove of firs form a deep green border on the side nearest to the County Infirmary and will eventually, one by one, be transferred from there to such spots, as may be in need of tree-ornamentation.

The technical management of the cemetery is entrusted to able hands, to the experienced superintendent, J. S. Birkeland, who for seventeen years acted as superintendent of Graceland cemetery, where he earned an enviable reputation and proved an important factor in the accomplishment of many valuable improvements.

Mount Olive is a Scandinavian Lutheran cemetery, but the privileges extended to those, wishing to lay to rest their deceased relatives, are not confined to Scandinavians or Lutherans alone; people of all creeds and nationalities, who are able and willing to conform to the rules and regulations laid down by the cemetery company, are permitted to bring the remains of their departed loved ones to this beautiful park cemetery, and take away the consoling thought, that they have left the form that no longer feels the vexations and struggles of life, in the midst of all this peaceful beauty.

A spacious receiving vault, built after the latest scientific formula and in connection therewith a fine Chapel have been erected, but the principal feature in the development of this "God's acre" consists in the natural facilities for drainage, secured by the remarkable elevation of the grounds. Land, so thoroughly drained, has no superior for cemetery purposes.

As already indicated, this cemetery is surrounded on all sides by a delightful and vast landscape. The many fine shade trees within the limits of Mount Olive with their rich foliage, turning into golden yellow, red and brown in autumn, tend to heighten the effect of the picturesque scenery in its entirety. The highest part of Mount Olive lies at an elevation of 18 feet above the level of the surrounding prairie, consequently the many handsome monuments adorning the cemetery can be noticed at some distance peeping through the leafy bowers of shrubs and trees.

The cemetery company was organized and received its charter in April, 1886. The License was issued to Paul O. Stensland, Frithjof Hjortdahl, Ole L. Stangeland, Andrew P. Johnson, Christian L. Benson. Hjalmar P. Brusewitz and Alfred Jacobson as Commissioners to open books for subscription to the capital stock of said company

The capital stock of the Scandinavian Lutheran Cemetery Association originally was twenty-five thousand dollars. Among the largest shareholders were: Paul O. Stensland, Bernt Anderson, A. P. Johnson, Ole L. Stangeland, Jens Olson, Jacob Johnson, John Eskilson, John Anderson, C. L. Benson, Louis Carlson, L. Branstad, G. Gabrielson, etc.

On the 10th day of April, 1886, the stockholders, in a meeting held for that purpose, proceeded to elect Directors for the term of one year, viz; Andrew P. Johnson, Alfred Jacobson, Paul O. Stensland, Ole L. Stangeland, Christian L. Benson, Benjamin F. Richolson and Severt T. Gunderson,

Of the officers elected at that time Mr. Paul O. Stensland, who was chosen Secretary and Treasurer, has been in active service ever since up to the present day and to his indefatigable and zealous activity is owing in a great measure the remarkable success, Mount Olive cemetery has achieved.

The Directors of the Cemetery Association now are: S. T. Gunderson President; Paul O Stensland, Secretary and Treasurer; Charles E. Schlytern, Soren D. Thorsen, Anker Stabford, Halvor Michelsen, and John Oleson.

Paul O. Stensland was born in Sandeid, Stavanger Amt, Norway, on May 9th, 1847. He grew up in the healthful surroundings of farm life in his native land and received his early elementary education in the schools of the district. At the age of eighteen years we find him leaving the family home and farm and traveling to Hindostan, in Peninsular Asia. In this new land he immediately connected himself with the cotton and wool industries of India and became a large buyer. For almost six years he traveled extensively through that country and at the same time acquired great knowledge and experience thereby. In the fall of 1870, he returned to his native country and during his short stay of three months both of his parents died. This sad family bereavment prompted Mr. Stensland to again leave his home and this time he chose Chicago as the field of his labors. He arrived here in the spring of 1871, and has resided here ever since. His first venture here was in the dry goods business, in 1885 he entered the real estate and insurance business and four years later he was sufficiently known and had gained the confidence and respect of his fellow citizens in such a degree, that he commenced a private banking business, in which he was so successful that in 1891 he changed this private bank to a State bank; of this, the Milwaukee Ave. State Bank, he is at present the president. Mr. Stensland is, as appears from the description of Mount Olive cemetery, the Secretary and Treasurer of this company and he also is the publisher of the Scandinavian newspaper 'Norden." For nine years, from 1879 to 1888, he was a member of the Board of Education of this city, in which he acquired a high reputation by his energy and executive ability in the discharge of his duties as member and chairman of some of the most important committees.

The former Mayor of this city, DeWitt C. Cregier, appointed him a member of a committee in connection with Washington Hesing, Ferd. Peck and General Fitz-Simons, for the purpose of revising the city charter of Chicago.

When Mr. James Scott, of the Chicago "Herald," resigned from the position as director of the World's Columbian Exposition, the vacancy was filled by the election of Mr. Stensland to the position. In April, 1892, he was reelected director. He is a member of the Iroquois Club and several Scandinavian societies.

View in Waldheim Cemetery.

BOHEMIAN NATIONAL CEMETERY.

The extreme north-western portion of our city, the Town of Jefferson, likewise possesses a number of cemeteries and near them people, to whom these cemeteries and the funeral corteges arriving and leaving furnish the means of subsistence. These people are the grave diggers, saloon-keepers, gardeners, manufacturers and dealers in monuments, etc.

The largest and most extensively used of these burying grounds is the Bohemian National Cemetery, situated about one mile from Irving Park in a north-easterly direction on Crawford Avenue. Here the pilgrim who has arrived at the end of life's journey, can enter without being questioned about his religion, color, or nationality. Equal rights are accorded to all. The immediate vicinity of this city of the dead is very charming, made so by the many pretty groves and other natural beauties the surrounding country possesses.

Since the Bohemian National Cemetery has been opened the whole neighborhood has greatly improved and all the property around has risen in value, especially after the region had been annexed to the city of Chicago. The place is but seven miles from the Court House, and will soon be connected with the center of the city by an electric railroad which the enterprising citizens of the 27th ward are going to build soon, having been incorporated for that purpose in September, 1892. This railroad will also connect the Insane Asylum of Cook County, and the Bohemian and Polish Catholic Cemetery with the city, and will greatly help in enlivening and settling this beautiful part of the city; here the Chicago River glides through beautiful fields and groves, having its water untarnished and not yet poisoned by the additions received farther on from so many shops and factories along its shores.

The cemetery was opened in the summer of 1877 and owes its existence to the freethinking half of the Bohemian population of Chicago. There were about 40,000 Bohemians in the city at that time, of whom about 25 per cent belonged to the Catholic church and the others where freethinkers, having a large congregation of Bohemian Freethinkers founded in 1871, called the "Svobodna Obec" and meeting at the large Bohemian Hall on Taylor street, that was destroyed by fire not long ago. The minister of this congregation was Frank B. Zdrubek, and the Catholics were led by their pastor, Rev. Jos. Molitor, at the St. Wenceslaus Church on Dekoven street.

In the year 1876 a discord of long duration broke out among the church members of the St. Wenceslaus' parish. Many persons who considered themselves good Catholics were prohibited from burying their relatives and members of their families in the Bohemian and Polish Catholic Cemetery, situated on Milwaukee avenue, about 13 miles from the Court House. The parson put forth different reasons for his actions which where not acceptable and did not seem reasonable to the Bohemians, and their discontent grew alarmingly, as the repeated refusals of burying caused great troubles and discords among the mourning relatives. To end all these disturbances, the Freethinkers convoked a mass meeting on January 7th, 1877, and there the foundation of the new organization for the purpose of building a Bohemian National Cemetery was laid. The beginnings were small and slow, but good will and earnest endeavor succeeded magnificently Many and great obstacles stood in the way of the undertaking, but all were overcome, and the cemetery, which originally had but 30 acres of ground has 50 acres now, and at this writing nearly 9,600 bodies sleep their eternal sleep there.

The organization began with but seven strong Bohemian Societies and Lodges and grew every year until it now counts 36 Lodges or Societies. Every

Society and Lodge sends two representatives to the Board of Managers, consisting now of 72 members who are mostly elected alternately from their societies for one and two years. The incorporation of the Board of Managers was signed at Springfield, Ill., April 11th, 1877.

Up to the present time about thirty acres of the entire area have been devoted to sepulture, and the superintendent deserves to be complimented for the excellent manner in which he performs his duties. The Board of Managers meet every two weeks at the Bohemian and English Free School building, No. 400 W. 18th street, and are untiring in working industriously for this undertaking, having no other remuneration but the thanks and — sometimes ingratitude of their societies. Some of the members of the management have served throughout these fifteen years faithfully without pay, deserving high acknowledgement for their labors and sacrifices in the interest of this great cause.

During the summer and autumn months the grounds represent a beautiful garden, artistically laid out and preserved by the skillful cemetery gardener, Mr. Leopold Ine, who takes good care of five green-houses in connection with the cemetery, devoting most of his time to artistic flori-culture, being especially clever and successful in bringing forth the rarest kinds of roses. How profitable the raising of flowers proves itself here, becomes evident from the fact that from the sale of flowers, the decoration of graves, and from watering the plants on these little mounds, no less than $6,600 was taken in during 1892. The five green-houses with all their improvements have cost $11.615 and the artesian wells $3,000.

As has been the case in the most other cemeteries, here too the beginning was made with stone copings and railings around graves, but several years ago the popular lawn system found favor with the Board of Managers and has happily now become the rule. Especially the western part of the cemetery is laid out in accordance with this system, and forms one of the most pleasant spots in the cemetery.

The management has very properly placed a great deal of importance and paid out large sums of money on the drainage and water systems, which are models of perfection, and have so far cost over $9,000. The walks and roads in the cemetery up to the present time involved an expenditure of $15.000. The first artesian well was sunk to a depth of 1610 feet, from which 250 gallons of pure and clear water gush forth each minute. All the property of the cemetery with its improvements amounts to $80,000, according to the last report of the financial committee. The Board of Managers devote a considerable portion of the clear profits of the undertaking to benevolent and educational purposes. They bury from 30 to 50 poor dead persons every year gratis, and allow besides other small gifts for charitable purposes, several hundred dollars for Bohemian and English free schools, of which there are five in the city of Chicago.

In 1885 a monument to Rev. Prof. Ladimir Klacel, a Bohemian philosopher and scholar who died at Belle Plaine, Ia., in 1883, was erected at a cost of $800 with the bust of the great freethinker faithfully carved in white marble by the sculptor Frank Hess of Irving Park. In the spring of 1892 a fine Soldiers' Monument was erected and dedicated, costing about $5,000. Many of the Bohemian Societies have taken steps leading to the erection of a Bohemian National Monument in this cemetery, for which space has been reserved in a large circular plat of the main driveway. There are quite a number of handsome and costly monuments scattered over this cemetery, upon which we read the names of the most prominent Bohemian families of Chicago.

The following are the officers for 1893: Vaclav Matas, President; Joseph Flora, Vice-President; Joseph Becvar, Corresponding Secretary; St. J. Halik, Financial Secretary; Joseph Babka, Treasurer; Joseph A. Smejkal, Joseph Sindelar, Frank Fucik, Board of Trustees; Joseph Kostner, Superintendent.

Bohemian National Cemetery.—Soldiers' Monument.

Other Sketches and Views.

Other Statutes and Views

P. S. PETERSON'S ROSE HILL NURSERY.

About a mile and a half west of the cemetery at Rosehill and the adjoining station of the Northwestern Railroad, in the midst of a charming stretch of country, is situated an extensive plantation full of interest to the friends of arboriculture and the lovers of Nature in general. This picturesque oasis in the wide plain given over to agricultural pursuits, covers an area of over four hundred acres and forms the well known Nursery of Mr. P. S. Peterson, which is not only the largest but also the oldest "tree-school" in the vicinity of Chicago, having been established by the present owner twenty-eight years ago, during which time it has furnished a very large number of the shade-trees and ornamental shrubs now adorning our public parks, cemeteries, residence streets, and private gardens. From this it may be inferred, that arboriculture is carried on here as a business enterprise, but notwithstanding this fact Mr. Peterson deserves to be ranked among the most prominent promoters of the public welfare, for without his ceaseless and highly successful labors upon the field of tree-growing for so many years, the people of our Metropolis would at the present day not be enabled to enjoy the blessings which are dispensed through the planting of foliage-trees and blooming shrubs upon our public grounds and streets, in such a large measure as is really and happily the case. Many thousands of the most beautiful trees in our parks: maple, linden, catalpas, elms, ash, poplars, etc, numberless shrubs and bushes, that cover themselves in the spring-time with a gay and festive mantle of sweet-scented flowers, received their first training at the hands of Mr. Peterson and his able assistants, at the head of which stands the only son of the proprietor, Mr. Wm. A. Peterson, a young gentleman of extensive knowledge and learning.

Among a people of culture and enlightenment planting and embellishing Nature herself, ranks among the first of public virtues. Gardening was probably one of the first arts that succeeded to that of building houses, but no doubt the term Garden for many centuries implied no more than a kitchen-garden or orchard. Then the custom of making square gardens enclosed with walls were established to the exclusion of nature and prospect and these gardens became selfish and sumptuous solitudes. To crown these impotent displays of false taste, the shears were applied to the lovely wildness of form with which Nature had distinguished each various species of tree and shrub; the compass and square were of more use in plantations than the landscape architect. Sir Henry Englefield was one of the first who saw the errors, the landscape gardeners of his time had fallen into and he selected with singular taste that chief beauty of all gardens, prospect and fortunate points of view. Prospects were before this sacrificed to convenience and warmth and since then the art of landscape gardening has made such rapid strides in the direction of discovering the point of perfection, that we may be justly proud of what has been achieved in softening Nature's harshnesses and copying her graceful touch.

But in forming ornamental plantations the selection of the proper species of trees and shrubs is a most important point. In the choice of trees, four things are observable: the height, the form, the color and the use. The latter is more essential to a good selection than may appear at first sight, nothing heightens the idea of ornament more than utility. Immediately under the eye, the gaudy shrub and the ornamental, though useless, Exotic may be admitted, but for more distant objects and in less embellished situations the Timber tree ought to prevail. There is harmony in taste, as in music; variety and even wildness, in its proper place, may be admitted, but discord ought not be allowed. Trees should not only be well chosen, but also well arranged and well planted. If that is done, it will soon be observed, that even grass and trees alone are capable of producing a wonderful richness and elegance.

The cheerful and inviting country-residence, in which Mr. Peterson dwells with his family, seems a suitable accompaniment to the stately trees, that embellish the recluse landscape, of which the delightful domicile of the proprietor forms the main attraction. No wonder that strangers that pass by pause to admire this rural scenery; and the liberality of Mr. Peterson is equal to his taste. His gratifications are heightened by those who seek enjoyment in his place; giving orders that nothing may be omitted which can increase their pleasure. The house throughout shows that it is the home of intellectual pursuits and refinement, being fully in harmony with the charming effect of the lofty grove without, whose fine old trees contribute not a little to make up an assemblage, which gives the mind ample food for reflection and great satisfaction to the eye.

There are a number of outhouses, of which the imposing and massive stable is the most conspicuous. It is inhabited by many fine draft and riding-horses, cows of the Jersey breed and also contains the wagons and coaches in use on the place. From this park the tree and shrub plantations extend in all directions; the plants may there be seen in endless straight rows like soldiers in line stretching as far as the eye can reach and producing charming effects with their various shapes and color-tints. With the view of laying down a crop destined to stand for generations, Mr. Peterson has taken every precaution to secure its vigor and success, by selecting plants of the most approved varieties of the species; he well understands the importance to obtain young plants grown from a good stock, or from the most approved trees of their kind. Another thing in which he excels is the process of transplanting large and heavy forest trees. Nowhere else has this branch of nursery-work been brought to such a high state of perfection. Trees that weighed from 15 to 20 tons and had attained the ripe age of 100 years, were successfully removed from their native soil and transplanted to new parts.

The growing of trees and shrubs on these lands is as a matter of course confined to the cultivation of such as are ornamental and suitable to climate and soil. The majority of the plants are propagated on the premises, some are imported from foreign countries and they comprise principally new or rare species, in fact mostly plants that may be classed among the latest achievements upon the field of tree and shrub-culture, and which possess all the qualities requisite to a successful growth as an ornamental tree in this section of our country. And what is very important, a rolling appearance can given to our flat landscape by the judicious arrangement of trees and shrubs of different sizes and shapes.

Taking a stroll through the extensive plantation, we find among the trees many kinds, that have a large number of family relations, all adapted to our climate and many of recent introduction; all promising to become valuable and ornamental.

While wandering about, with Mr. Peterson as our guide, let us make brief notes of some of the best known and most popular ornamental trees and shrubs that present themselves to our notice.

The *Mountain Ash* is a well-known beautiful tree with smooth branches and the leaves pinnate, with uniform, serrate, smooth leaflets. The beauty of its foliage is hardly surpassed by any other deciduous tree.

The tall or common *Ash* attains to a great size, reaching in fine specimens to about 100 feet. It possesses a very elegant figure and forms during summer a very desirable object in lawn or park scenery.

The chief use of the *Linden* or Lime tree is to form an embowering shade along avenues and as a park tree or lawn ornament. In Scotland on the lawn at Gordon Castle stands a Linden tree with a head of nearly 100 feet and a trunk of over 16 feet in diameter. Our American Linden is of a more robust habit than the European tree.

View in Waldheim.

The whole genus of *Maple* is remarkably handsome and some of the species grow rapidly at an early age in almost any soil. Many kinds are interesting on account of their flowering early at the time of the expansion of the foliage; and from their elegantly-lobed leaves, of the finest texture, which in autumn furnish the most exquisite tints of every shade of yellow and scarlet, they are highly prized in ornamental plantations.

The *Elm* (Ulmus americana) is a tall elegant tree of rapid growth. From the density of its foliage and its clustering habit of growth in bright weather it displays a variety of light and shade such as painters appreciate in such objects.

The *Poplar* tree, like the Willows, is unisexual—either a male or female plant. The poplar trees are remarkable for rapidity of growth and therefore they are frequently employed to furnish immediate effect in a bare locality.

Among ornamental *Willows* the Salix Babylonica (Weeping Willows) forms a very graceful and interesting tree, but the American varieties have a higher value on account of their being extremely hardy. Their long slender twigs droop down with much elegance and become agitated by the slightest impulse of the wind, like the spray of a playing fountain. The Mahogany-willow, coming from France, with its bright red stem and branches makes a warm and attractive addition to our cold and long winters.

The *Birch*, adapting itself to various soils and situations, possesses a wider range than any other plant. There are some very fine weeping birches, espe-cially the cut-leaved, which add a graceful variety of verdure to scenes in them-selves beautiful.

The *Alder* in a cultivated state and in good soil attains to a considerable size and often becomes very picturesque in figure and displays a ramification little inferior to that of the oak.

Considered as an ornament few trees attract more attention than the *Beech*. Its stem is massive and powerful, its bark is smooth and of a silvery cast, and when the heat of summer unfolds its silken foliage, it displays a ver-dure of softness and delicacy and when viewed in the park, amidst the sun-shine and showers of summer time, it is a gem indeed.

The weeping Beech is a very valuable and ornamental tree and so is the out-leaved weeping beech, which is one of the most elegant pendulous trees in cultivation. It has the advantage of at once assuming the pendulous habit of growth.

The *Norway Spruce* is also of great beauty, of very uniform growth and, when allowed sufficient space in a congenial soil, it retains even at an advanced age, its branches and luxuriant foliage.

The *Pine* tree tribe is too well known to need any description. It con-sists of evergreen trees, natives of Europe, Asia and America, and is perhaps one of the most valuable of any genus of ligueous plants.

The *Sycamore* grows to a great height and ample size, throwing out a wide-spread top. Its leaves are vine-shaped. Hanbury says, the Sycamore being wounded exudes a great quantity of liquor, of which is made good wine. There are three varieties of the Sycamore.

The beautiful *Catalpa* will grow to a height of 40 or 50 feet, anc as the leaves are fine and large, it should be planted as a standard in the midst of fine openings, but these should be such as are well sheltered, for the leaves, being quite large, make such a resistance to the summer's high winds, as to occasion whole branches to be split off by that powerful element. Of great beauty are the white flowers breaking open late in the Spring and adding in a great measure to the elegance of this handsome shade-tree.

The *Snow-drop tree* or white Fringe tree, a native of Virginia, will grow to the height of about fifteen feet. Its leaves are large, shaped like a laurel, broad and roundish, and the flowers of a pure white, come out in bunches, in May, from every part of the tree.

As an ornamental tree *Chestnut* also has a degree of greatness belonging to it which recommends it strongly to the gardeners attention.

The *Hydrangea* seldom grows to more than a yard or four feet high and affords as much pleasure to those who delight in fine flowers as it does to the botanist. The leaves are a great ornament to these plants; being very large and having their upper surface of a fine green and their under rather downy. But the flowers constitute the greatest beauty of these plants, for they are produced in very large bunches in August. Their color is white and the end of every bunch will be ornamented with them. They have an agreeable odor and make such a show altogether, as to distinguish themselves even at a considerable distance.

Of the shrubbery *St. John's Wort*, or Hypericum, there are several varieties, one of which will grow to a height of eight feet. The flowers are yellow and make a good show in June and July and are succeeded by oval black-colored capsules, containing ripe seeds in the autumn.

The deciduous *Privet* (Ligustrum Vulgare) will grow to a height of about ten or twelve feet. The dark green leaves continue on the tree very late and the flowers, which are white and very beautiful, are succeeded in the autumn by black berries, which at that season constitute the greatest beauty of the plant.

The black and garden *Mulberry* is principally cultivated for the fruit and in ornamental plantations a few of them will be sufficient to make the collection general.

The two thorned *Acacia* (Robinia) gets its leaves late in the Spring, but for this it makes ample amends by the beautiful foliage it will display soon after. But its greatest beauty it receives from its flowers, which are produced in long pendulous bunches in June, their color is white.

The *Locust* tree (false Acacia) grows very rapidly in rich, dry, well sheltered soil and becomes a tree of considerable height.

The *Laburnum* is the largest species of the very ornamental genus Cytisus. It is a low deciduous tree with trifoliate leaves.

The *Elder* tree comprehends several species and has been known medicinally from the earliest period of our medicinal history.

Besides those mentioned we also find many elegant species of Clematis, Ivy, Jasmine, Honeysuckle, Magnolia, Syringa, Sumach, Rose bushes, Lilac, Spiræa, Arbor Vitæ, Viburnum, Calycanthus, Mock Orange, Bignonia, Virginia Creeper, Nightshade, etc.

Naturally there are not a few of the shrubs which find it very difficult to thrive and keep up a healthy growth in smoky factory-districts; others again can ill endure cold winds, while another class will demand a sunny location to ripen out its twigs and a fourth a position with plenty of shade; such conditions can be found many more. In laying out parks, gardens or cemeteries it is of the utmost importance to make a wise selection of shrubs and to place them in positions, where they will grow and become an object of delight to the beholder. Especially is this true in regard to cemeteries. There the gardener can produce much more pleasing effects and impressions, than the sculptor with masterpieces of his art.

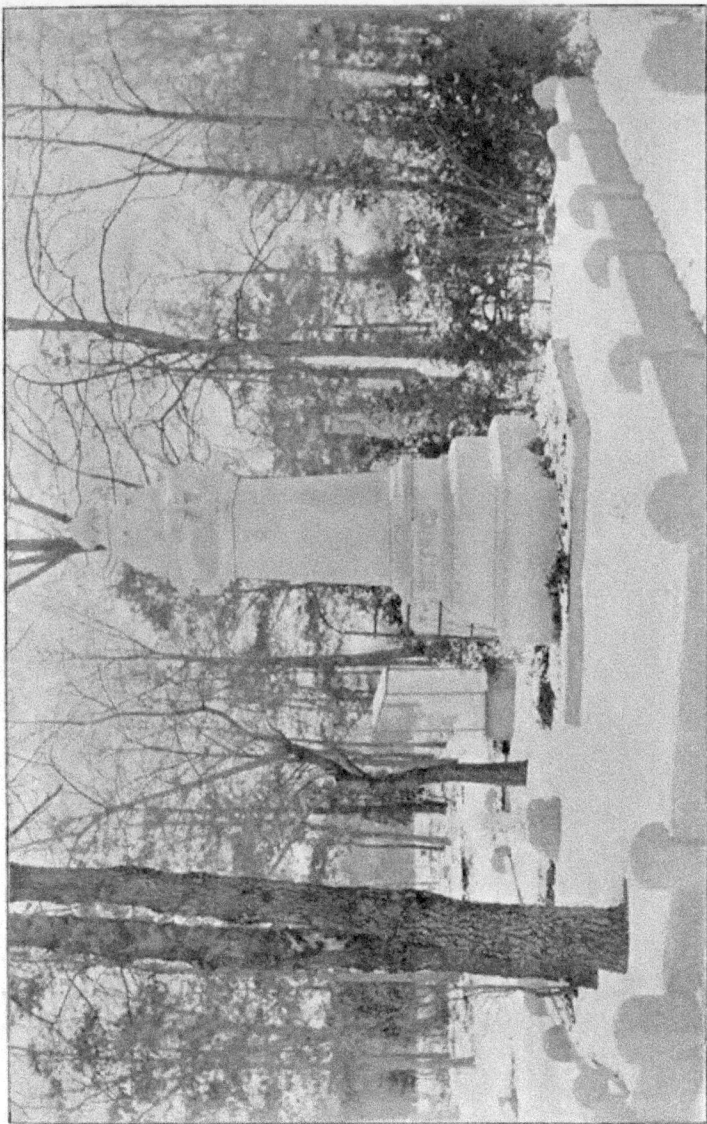

Scene in Waldheim.

EGANDALE.

The prevailing disposition among the people of the eastern cities to turn away from the overcrowded and inconvenient summer-resorts and seek recreation and repose in country-homes of their own, is rapidly taking hold of their brethren in the western states, but instead of having to choose worn-out, abandoned farms, like many of those in the New England states are, where natural scenery alone atones for the shortcomings indicated, "Chicagoites" have within easy reach of their city homes and business places a section of country, full of scenic beauty—where picturesque woodlands and water-views, fern-clad dells and velvety lawns vie with each other in well asserted claims for genuine admiration.

Commencing just north of our city and bordering Lake Michigan for forty miles or more is a magnificent stretch of land yet largely in its primeval beauty. Gradually rising, the surface extending northward culminates in a height of about ninety feet, forming at the shore-line bold and precipitous bluffs. From Winetka north to Waukegan for quite a distance landward the surface is ramified by heavily wooded ravines, gradually growing deeper as they approach the lake and widening out until they represent a "sunken forest" of considerable area. At Highland Park, these ravines are at their best and within the last few years many of Chicago's prominent citizens have here selected sites for summer-homes. Here the surface is gently undulating, forming numerous knolls, from which enchanting scenic-effects are everywhere visible; commanding views of the lake, with a sail or two mostly always in sight, for along this shore the great commerce of the lake passes on its way north and south; magnificent ravine-pictures, showing the feathery tree-tops, springing from a low level, nod their plumes as a greeting to the passing breeze, thus calming and quieting the mind through the medium of our vision.

The most conspicuous points of landscape-beauties are rapidly being taken for human habitations and many costly improvements of this kind are under way. We choose for the purpose of illustrating some of the natural beauties of this north-shore paradise with its glades and groves and cool secluded nooks "Egandale," a typical and model summer home, where peace and repose reign supreme, where rural, rustic beauty exerts its soothing and refreshing influence. The broad vine-clad verandah suggests a cool retreat indeed during the mid-day hours. From this leafy bower is seen as charming a water-view, as some of the most renowned lakes of this country can boast of. A roadway near by, descending a ravine bank on its way to the lake some eighty feet below, cuts through the overlapping trees, through which is visible, embowered in emerald-green, the merrily dancing waters over the partly submerged pebbled shore—and by a lucky chance the bright light of the rising harvest-moon is spread out over the path of this vision and illuminates the rippling surface with its silvery fleece.

Egandale consists of five and a half acres, nearly one-third of which is composed of wooded ravines. A main ravine forms the southern and western boundary line and small sub-ravines extend into the tableland—thus forming lovely bays and other points of interest. Being heavily wooded they act as shrubbery belts to hide and mask "surprises," which the wanderer constantly meets with—be it a rustic bridge, or a vine-covered bower, or some unexpected enchanting lake-view—there are many of them. One lake-view is particularly fine, where from a point, looking over the main ravine eighty feet deep, which here makes an abrupt turn, a broad expanse of water is seen over the tree-tops. The trees of the upper portion of the banks form a V-shaped frame for the pictures and here again is seen the rising moon with all its accompanying glory.

We have room for only a few illustrations of the many interesting spots of this summer-home. The "Rockery" speaks for itself as a good illustration of what can be accomplished in this department of landscape work. The "Basket"-picture shows part of the lawn—the ravine trees bounding it on the south—the "Rockery," in the distance, in a line with the "Basket," and the roadway leading to the lake.

Example.—Porch Decoration

DOMESTIC CONSERVATORIES.

There are degrees of beauty in the leaves of plants; and while it is not reasonable to suppose that any one cultivator can find accommodation for all the choice Exotics which are to be found in the principal gardens of this country or Europe, it is quite reasonable to conclude that from want of space he would be compelled to make a selection, retaining only those which most commend themselves to his admiration, either on account of their bold and striking or distinct character, or from their delicacy and beauty.

Amateur plant growers have everywhere largely increased during the last few years and the collection of plants they cultivate is a proof that their conception of the beautiful is not confined to brilliant colored flowers alone, but that they are able to appreciate grace and elegance in the form and markings of the leaves, independent of bloom, which has been for so many years the sole aim of the horticulturist. But although the beautiful-leaved plants are exceedingly ornamental and gay when grouped together by themselves, a judicious selection from both classes, according to the space at disposal, is the surest means of producing a gay and cheerful effect throughout the entire year.

As a well known writer says: "For so many years it was the sole aim of the horticulturist to look forward to the development of flowering plants as the sole reward of a whole seasons labor Now, however, we live in happier times, and derive a greater share of pleasure from our plants, because we grow and prize many which have beautifully variegated or otherwise richly ornamented leaves. How it was, that we were so long learning to love these highly ornamental plants, it is difficult to say; but we are becoming thoroughly alive now to the noble and massive beauty displayed by some, to the graceful and elegant outlines of others and to the richness and singularity in the colors and markings of the leaves of many more."

The love of the beautiful in nature, from a pansy to a forest oak, is deeply implanted in the human breast, and constitutes a source which requires only to be reached and acted upon in order to diffuse on every side innumerable advantages to individuals and to society. We see the love of plants and flowers existing, apparently under the most discouraging circumstances, and in spots where poverty chokes almost all the springs of wholesome pleasure. It is pitiable to see these sickly objects of care in the pent-up city pining under the influence of the dry atmosphere; and deep must be the inherent taste which can persevere in resisting the obstacles to healthy vegetation, caused by deleterious matter floating constantly in the air, the excess of aridity or moisture, excessive heat and cold, sudden alternations of temperature, and nipping blasts from over the level plains.

Against these destructive influences, the green-house or conservatory, which formerly was regarded as exclusively the appendage of the stately mansion, or the suburban residences of the opulent, is a protection. The domestic green-house has been made an inexpensive means of gratifying a taste, which, while it is at once refined and elegant, excites an inquisitive spirit that raises those who are fortunate enough to be under its influence, above low and frivolous pursuits.

The exclusion of particles of soot and other noxious matter adapts the green-house for the city as well as the country, and we may select any space of sufficient size in which to build our green-house and bid the plants of tropical regions flourish in the most unpropitious spots in the heart of Chicago. In prisons, men have solaced themselves for the loss of liberty by the visits of a spider or a mouse, whose motions they have studied and watched with delight; but here is a study open to a great many of those who enjoy the comforts of a home, which is pregnant with the most admirable results, at once gratifying the eye and informing the mind and opening a page of the book of nature to the dweller of the city.

The foregoing must not lead the reader to the belief, that a treatise on greenhouse-gardening and plant-culture is to follow. That is left to those who possess the necessary qualifications and knowledge of plants.

The subject presented itself to the author during his visits to several of the most complete private collections of plants under glass-roofs in this city and among them none have obtained a greater celebrity than the plant-houses of the gentlemen named in the pages following. These men have spared neither time nor money in gathering together from almost every quarter of the world some of the most wonderful and remarkable productions of the vegetable kingdom.

ADOLPH SCHÖNINGER'S CONSERVATORY AND GARDEN.

Mr. Adolph Schöninger is one of the few Chicagoans that have realized their youthful ideals. They had clung to him; he had never deviated from the programme he had mapped out in his mind many years ago. And later he set about putting them in concrete shape. For a number of years he had found untold pleasure in horticulture and hot-house gardening at his residence, and recently, with practically illimitable means at his disposal, he resolved to realize his boldest dream. So he bought a large plat of desirable property on Melrose Street, way out in Lake View, midway between Evanston Avenue and the lake. And on this he laid out a spacious garden and built him a fine house—commodious, just to his taste.

And then he proceeded to build, adjacent to and directly connecting with the house, a fine and large private conservatory. And it is this conservatory and the propagating houses belonging to it which are worthy of a description. Among the 1,500 kinds of foliage plants, flowers and fruit-trees represented in the green and hot houses under the care of a gardener, there are a hundred or more of the rarest and costliest. Some new varieties have been propagated by his own skill, and a few of these are as yet not generally known to florists, and are still awaiting baptismal ceremonies.

It is in the matter of orchids, those eccentric and luxurious children of the tropics, that this conservatory is especially rich. The collection comprises several hundreds of them, and among them are a score or more of very rare ones. The dining-room connects with the conservatory by a broad, high glass door which is generally left open. Entering through it a scene of surpassing vernal beauty meets the eye. A balmy air, slightly saturated with grateful moisture, fills the lungs. All around and over-head blossoms of deep tint give out a rich fragrance, and the eye feasts on the graceful, feathery foliage of palms and ferns. In a small but pretty aviary birds of tropical plumage hop and chirp and sing, and an aquarium of handsome design is alive with glistening goldfishes and other creatures that love the water as their native element, while pinky shells and ferns of softest green make a harmonious color-effect about them. The foot treads on a smooth, polished surface of stone, and through the glass doors beyond a glimpse of still rarer and more delicate plant life is had. As we look down these long lines of fantastic vegetation, glorying under the beams of a burning sun, and wrapped in a bath of humid half-suffocative air, it requires no great stretch of the imagination to conceive ourselves translated to those tropical countries where nature at play laughs at the rules to which she succumbs in our own more temperate country.

Amidst the noble palm-trees the mind is struck with a feeling almost of awe. He must be apathetic, indeed, whose thoughts are not elevated in such a scene. Well did Linnaeus call palms the princes of the vegetable world; the beautiful character of their crown of leaves amply justifies the title. The species of palms and other plants found in Mr Schöninger's houses are nearly all of them dwellers of the other plant-houses named in these pages and can be

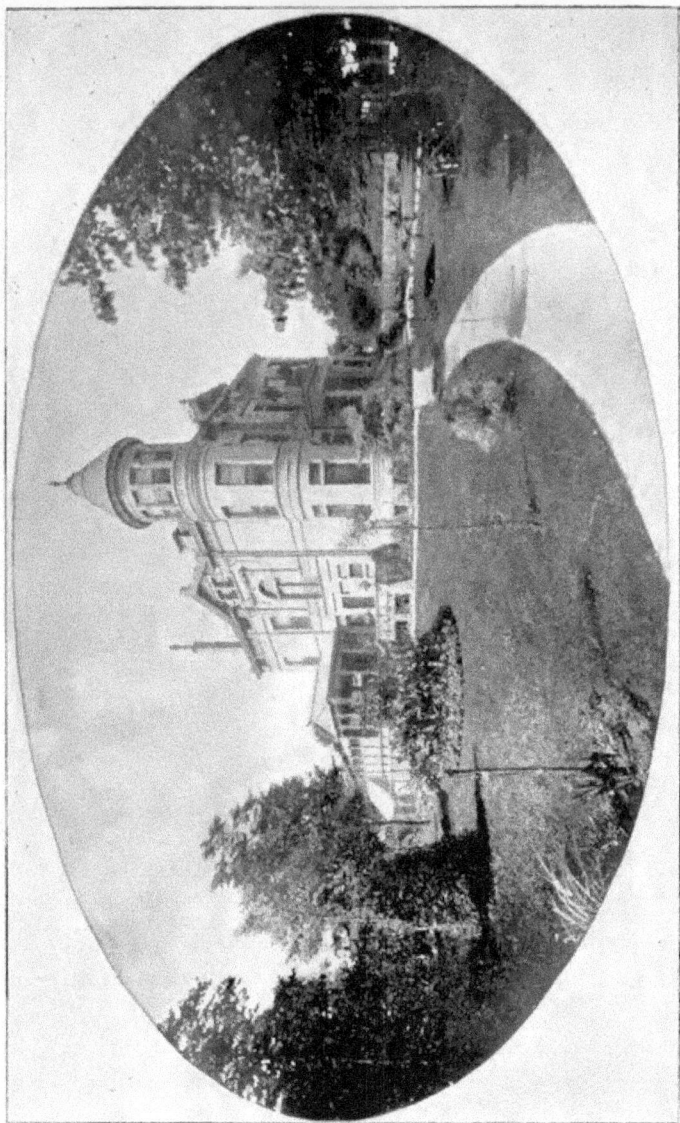

Residence and Conservatory of Adolph Schöninger,

admired by any respectable person, who may apply for admission to any one of these conservatories.

Mr. Schöninger has rendered his conservatory pleasing by selecting principally ornamental plants of robust constitution, with green leaves of different shades or variegated and stout in texture. There are among a host of others: Palms, Dracaenas, Ferns, Begonias, Agaves, Yuccas, Anthuriums, Aralias, Crotons, Rhododendrons, Pelargoniums, Gloxinias, Geraniums, Fuchsias, bulbous plants in great variety, Camellias, etc.

During the summer months Mr. Schöninger divides his early summer morning hours and the time after his return from his factory between the conservatory and his many outdoor plants, which latter, on account of their being spread and scattered over a large piece of territory, require a great deal of care and nurturing. This garden is a beauty indeed, with its handsome floral decorations, its artistically embellished lily-pond, its stately trees and shrubs, forming in all a very appropriate assemblage for the elegant house in their midst.

EDWARD UIHLEIN'S CONSERVATORY.

To the friends of nature, who on their excursions to the parks make use of the street car-lines, the horse-railway on North Avenue offers a most desirable means of reaching Humboldt Park after having paid a visit to Lincoln Park, or to those who desire to go from Humboldt Park to the park on the North Side, for the cars of said line form a welcome connection between those two pleasure-gardens. They pass by Wicker Park, a finely ornamented square, or rather triangle, with beautiful trees, lawns, walks, ponds, etc, surrounded on all sides by handsome private residences, many of these having pretty little flower-gardens in front, by which the owners or tenants of the houses evince their love of flowers in a marked degree. But foremost among these friends of the children of Flora stands Mr. Edward Uihlein, one of the vice-presidents of the Chicago Horticultural Society, a gentleman of fine tastes and great popularity, and one who commands the honor and respect of all who have the good fortune of being acquainted with him.

Mr. Uihlein resides on Ewing Place, between Robey Street and Hoyne Avenue, where he and his family occupy a palatial residence that stands on the western end of a large park-like garden, richly but at the same time very tastefully embellished with flowers, shrubs and shade-trees. In the rear of these grounds and in close proximity to the family residence are situated the highly interesting greenhouses of Mr. Uihlein, which contain a collection of plants equal if not superior to any other private collection in this city. On these plants Mr. Uihlein bestows a great amount of loving care and under his judicious and skilled treatment they thrive and prosper like grateful children under the influences of affectionate parents. The total space devoted to the indoor-culture of flowers and plants covers an area of 34x56 feet and occupies an elevation high enough to furnish flowing water to a grotto of stalagmite situated in front of the pavilion-like conservatory. A neat fountain and a small goldfish-pond are attractive appendages of the warm-house filled with a wealth of rare and beautiful plants.

The greatest interest is awakened by the superb collection of orchids that are partly suspended from the glass roofs of the greenhouses, partly found in pots along the tiers below.

The arrangement of the plants is pretty much after the natural system and each has a label with its correct botanical name. The terrestrial orchids are mostly placed in flower pots, filled with appropriate soil and these are in some cases put upon other empty pots to secure the drainage, while the epiphytes or air-plants are all supported in the air in a manner diversified and curious.

Several of the superb tribe cattleya, named after an ardent admirer and cultivator of orchideous plants, were in full bloom during the author's visit, many of them emitting a fragrance which, added to their pre-eminent loveliness, makes them orchids of great esteem. One brilliant flower perfumed an area of many feet around it with a scent like verbena. The mimic powers are not confined to form, but extend also to the odor of other vegetable productions. For instance there is a dusky tiger-spotted plant whose flower exhales a delicious smell like that of raspberries; another sad-colored flower of very graceful drooping inflorescence possesses a scent precisely like that of the scented geranium.

Then there is the Pitcher-Plant, a native of Ceylon and a wonderful vagary of nature. The stem is erect and of a brownish color and the leaves are long and spear-shaped; the end of the central rib being lengthened out and sustaining the pitcher by being attached to the bottom of it. Were the pitcher cut off and exhibited to any person unacquainted with the existence of such a vegetable structure, when he examined its rougher, leathery, spotted exterior, its firm and rounded lip, so artificially marked in green and red, and its accurately-adapted lid, he would most probably unhesitatingly pronounce it to be an artificial production. A little sourish water, supposed to be secreted by the inner surface of the organ, is occasionally found in the pitcher. There are several varieties of this plant, the most popular of which seems the *Nepenthes distillatoria*.

Baskets containing the magnificent class of orchids called *Stanhopea* also hang from the roof of said houses. Their peculiarity consists in the production of their flowers from the roots, which are of a large size, and beautiful texture and coloring.

Among the extra-tropical orchids we find here the *Oncidium* tribe; the flowers of some of these species exhale a most sweet fragrance. Then there is a plant called the *Cypripedium*, which represents a large brown spider on its flower. It is an American species and the spider whose form it portrays is said by Linnaeus "to be capable of destroying insects and even small humming-birds."

And now a word or two in a by-the-way manner upon the peculiarities of orchideous plants. Artificially they are divisible into two classes—the terrestrial, which grow in or upon the soil; and the epiphytal, which grow upon the trunks or branches of trees, rocks and stones. The latter are the most curious from the fact that they derive their nourishment not from the soil, or as parasitical plants do from the sap of the trees on which they are found, but from the air. They have been called from this peculiarity "air plants" and present us with a phenomenon which was inexplicable until the researches of Liebig proved that plants, even growing in the soil, derive the principal portion of their solid constituent, wood, from the atmosphere. They extend long whitish roots abroad into the air as other plants do into the earth, by which they derive their necessary food. It is an appearance well calculated to surprise the mind, to see great masses of vegetation, as are some of the plants before us, feeding and luxuriating in the atmosphere, the carbonic acid gas of which is their chief support.

The general appearance and structure of orchids is a perfect anomaly. In their native countries they are to be found crawling over the trunks and branches of forest trees, climbing to their topmost boughs and squatting just where the limbs are united to the parent trunk, where they drop down clusters of flowers, of which one is puzzled to say which is the most striking—their beauty, grotesque appearance, or exquisite fragrance. The flowers are and have long been the puzzle and admiration of every botanist.

Not the least of the peculiarities of orchids lies in their disposition to mimic many natural objects; there is scarcely any animate being to which the flowers are not comparable. With the most artistic skill, to speak playfully, of the most ludicrous character, they imitate insects, lizards, frogs, birds, animals and even the human "face and form divine." From the roof of the greenhouses they depend in rows; many of these plants are in bloom successively at every period of the year.

And now let us take a look at some of the more conspicuous ornamental plants found in this collection. Following Mr. Uihlein, who kindly consented to act as our guide and expounder, our attention is particularly directed to the following species:

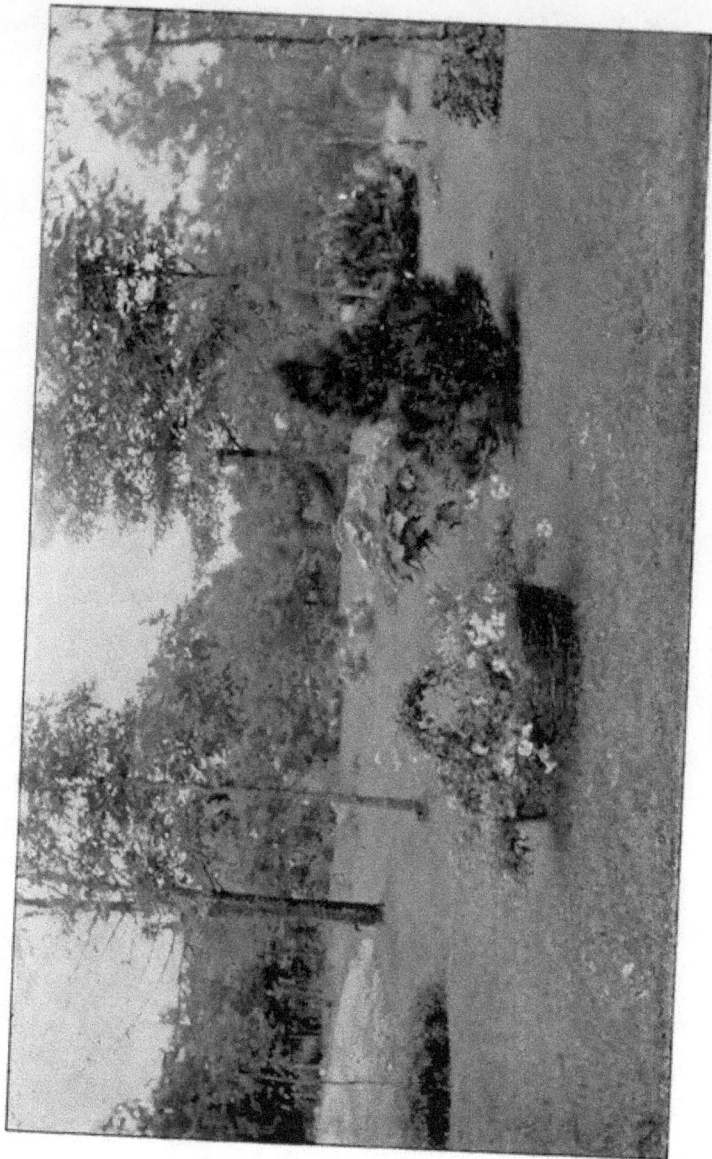

Egandale.—The "Flower Basket."

Areca, a genus of elegant pinnate-leaved Palms; *Aralia*, one of the most ornamental genus, is well adapted either for the conservatory or the open air in summer; *Alocasia*, plants of great beauty with large sagittate leaves and rich coloring; *Begonias*, which are not only remarkable for their free-flowering qualities but also for the exquisite variegation of their foliage; *Chamaedorea*, a genus of Palms with rich shining green and elegant pinnate leaves; *Cocos*, graceful and shade-loving plants of a noble order, of which one species yields the well known fruit—the cocoa-nut; *Carludovica*, Palm-like plants, which are often grown as Palms, but belong to the Cyclanth division of the Pandanads; *Corypha*, a genus which contains but few species, but some of them produce very large fan-leaves. They are plants of extremely slow growth and are characterized by tall, stout, cylindrical trunks; *Crotons*, are almost indispensable for the decoration of greenhouses or public exhibition, as their habit and color produce an effect, which is not produced by any other plant; *Cycas*, very handsome plants, are closely related to the Conifers and Ferns and are exceedingly useful for greenhouse decoration; *Dieffenbachia*, a very handsome plant; some species have yellowish green leaves from twelve to fifteen inches in length, irregularly blotched with dark green and profusely spotted with white; *Dracaenas*, plants that are amongst the most useful and beautiful of fine-foliaged plants of graceful habit, with beautifully colored leaves; *Kentia*, a genus of handsome, robust, greenhouse Palms; *Latania*, another handsome family of Palms with large fan-like leaves; *Maranta*, a plant-family that have their foliage more or less variegated, some of them in the most beautiful manner; few plants can equal them as objects of delight in a greenhouse collection; *Pandanus* or Screw Pines, plants that show a very peculiar spiral arrangement of their leaves and which in a state of nature grow twenty and thirty feet high; *Phoenix*, a genus of Palms and a very interesting and ornamental plant; the flower spikes are produced from amongst the leaves and not below them, male and female flowers being produced on separate plants; *Ptychosperma*, another exceedingly handsome genus of Palms, which in their natural state grow from ten to eighty feet in height; *Seaforthia*, a most graceful species of the Palm family and eminently well adapted for greenhouse decoration; *Tillandsia*, a genus of Bromeliaceous plants, containing many species remarkable for the beauty of their flowers; *Anthurium*, a plant highly valuable as a foliage plant with large leaves of a bold and striking character and with flowers of a brilliant shining scarlet color; *Billbergia*, a noble, and erect-growing species, and a very showy plant; *Vriesia*, an exceedingly handsome species of dwarf habit of growth; *Azalea*, a superb genus of highly ornamental plants, has become a great favorite and is much in favor as a decorative plant for indoor use; *Camellia*, a magnificent genus of evergreen shrubby plant with beautiful rose-like but odorless flowers; *Erica*, a very attractive greenhouse plant, that is much admired; *Rhododendron*, a well known and deservedly popular genus of many species. Besides those named there are numerous other families of plants, as for instance: Carissa, Cyeas, Euterpe, Aspidistra, many beautiful Ferns, Selaginella, Peristeria, Aerides, Saccolabium, Vanda, Angraecum, etc., all forming a most enjoyable group for the admiring eye of the flower-loving laymen as well as for the botanist.

J. C. VAUGHAN'S GREEN HOUSES.

Among the prominent and successful commercial gardeners of this city Mr. J. C. Vaughan stands in the front rank. His success may be attributed mainly to the firm stand he has taken, not to offer anything to his customers that is not meritorious or which is merely a fictitious and over-estimated curiosity under the name of "Novelty."

The greenhouses of Mr. Vaughan are situated at Western Springs, a beautiful suburb of Chicago, on the Chicago, Burlington & Quincy Railroad. They contain over 35,000 feet of glass and hot beds and cold frames in proportion. The frost-proof storage house for dormant Roses, Clematis, Dahlias and small fruits forms a valuable feature for the careful handling of such plants. Over this storage cellar are the Gladiolus and Tuberose bins and racks and the general packing room for mail and express orders. The greenhouses, sixteen in all, are devoted to the various plants as follows: Two large palm houses, one being 24 x 120 feet and 13 feet high, containing many magnificent plants, which will be grown for the World's Fair; one large house 18 x 150 feet, devoted to the new French Canna's, among them some beautiful new, unnamed seedlings; another house to Chrysanthemums, new and old, over 100 unnamed seedlings being grown for a thorough test before sending out; also five houses used exclusively for Roses, two of them 18 x 120 feet; two houses for bedding plants; a house for seed-testing; one for bulbs and tuberous rooted plants; two houses for propagating.

The Chrysanthemums put on exhibition at the Flower-shows in Chicago and other western cities were very creditable to the green-house department of Mr Vaughan's extensive business (he received eleven first premiums and two second prizes out of 13 entries at the second-last Chicago Flower-show), and they proved a delight to many of Mr. Vaughan's patrons, of which quite a number were fortunate enough to witness the far better display made at the greenhouses themselves. The central latitude provides a climate and seasons for varieties of plants suitable to the great agricultural belt of the Northern States, avoiding the small and inferior vegetables, flowers and grains from the extreme North, as well as the late, large-growing and non-maturing varieties of the South.

The *main store* at Nos. 146-148 West Washington Street in this city, occupies three floors, each 40 x 185 feet, and two cellars, the latter for potatoes. These storage, packing and shipping floors, with the facilities at Western Springs for storing duplicate stocks of bulbs, dormant Roses, Clematis, etc, are unexcelled for that purpose. The *city store* is in the center of the retail business of Chicago, at No. 88 State Street and will be found most convenient to all who make their purchases in person. At both stores can also be found garden and farm tools and supplies in endless variety.

It may be mentioned in addition to the above, that Mr. Vaughan intends to keep open house during this year. He is having printed a programme of the Horticultural Department of the World's Fair, its plan, its rules, its special features and seasonable shows in all departments. Part of this will appear in his regular 1893 catalogue, additional in bulletins as needed. All regular costumers and all new ones of this year will receive free the book for 1893 and also the bulletins issued concerning the Fair.

For the convenience of Eastern costumers, Mr. Vaughan has opened a store at No 12 Barclay Street, New York City, from where all seeds, bulbs, tools and supplies offered in the catalogues can be secured.

* * *

Besides the conservatories and green houses described in the foregoing there are in this city a number of other handsome private collections of plants, among which the collections of orchids in the conservatories of Wm. H. Chadwick, Potter Palmer, Dr. Clarke, G. Wittbold and others deserve special mention. And after our stroll through these conservatories we have not seen half of their contents; but after all how minute a portion do all of them, the horticultural and floricultural show at the World's Fair and the richly stocked palm-houses of our great parks included, constitute of that exhaustless treasure which enriches our globe! We had it undoubtedly strongly impressed upon our mind during the time that we held converse not with inanimate, insensate creatures, but with beings which delighted in the tender care that fed and fostered them, and exhibited their gratitude in language unintelligible only to those who have no heart to open, and no ears to give to such things.

J. C. Vaughan's Greenhouses at Western Springs.

THE QUEEN OF AQUATICS.

The public visiting Lincoln and Washington Parks owe a debt of gratitude to the men standing at the head of floriculture in these parks for having introduced to lovers of the beautiful in nature the queenly water-lily Victoria Regia, perhaps the most extraordinary of all floral productions. Lincoln Park was the first in this city to successfully rear this lily of the Amazon from seeds and Washington Park was not long in imitating the praiseworthy example set by its lovely sister on the North Side. In both parks the lily-ponds now form one of the chief attractions and there the great Victoria Regia reigns supreme over her numerous family relations of various complexions—all of them beautiful, however.

Although discovered by Professor Haenke, a German botanist of great repute, as early as 1801, it was not until 1837 that any historical sketch and description of the wonderful lily appeared. It was then again discovered, this time by Sir Robert Schomburgh, who transmitted the original drawings and a description to the London Botanical Society.

Mr. Schomburgh says: "It was on the 1st of January, 1837, while contending with the difficulties that nature interposed in different forms to stem our progress up the river Berbice (lat. 4°, 30′ N., long. 52° W.), that we arrived at a part where the river expanded and formed a currentless basin. Some object on the southern extremity of this basin attracted my attention, and I was unable to form an idea of what it could be; but, animating the crew to increase the rate of their paddling, we soon came opposite the object which had raised my curiosity, and, behold, a vegetable wonder! All calamities were forgotten; I was a botanist, and felt myself rewarded! There were gigantic leaves, five to six feet across, flat, with a broad rim; lighter green above, and vivid crimson below, floating upon the water; while, in character with the wonderful foliage, I saw luxuriant flowers, each consisting of numerous petals, passing, in alternate tints, from pure white to rose and pink. The smooth water was covered with the blossoms, and as I rowed from one to the other, I always found something new to admire. The flower-stalk is an inch thick near the calyx, and studded with elastic prickles about three-quarters of an inch long. When expanded, the four-leaved calyx measures a foot in diameter, but is concealed by the expansion of the hundred-petalled corolla. This beautiful flower, when it first unfolds, is white, with a pink centre; the color spreads as the bloom increases in age, and, at a day old, the whole is rose-colored. As if to add to the charm of this noble water-lily, it diffuses a sweet scent. As in the case of others in the same tribe, the petals and stamens pass gradually into each other, and many petaloid leaves may be observed bearing vestiges of an another. The seeds are numerous and imbedded in a spongy substance. Ascending the river we found this plant frequently; and the higher we advanced, the more gigantic did the specimens become; one leaf we measured was 6 feet 5 inches in diameter, the rim 5½ inches high and the flowers 1¼ feet across."

When the great American water-lily became known in Europe, a strong desire to obtain its introduction to that country in a living state soon evinced itself. After a series of futile attempts, the queen of all the lilies was successfully introduced into the Exotic Aquarium at Kew in England. A number of healthy plants being raised, one of them was sent to the gardens at Chatsworth, the seat of the Duke of Devonshire; and on the 1st of November, 1849, a flower appeared, indicating a condition of advancement beyond what had been attained by any of the other plants at Kew or elsewhere.

Professor Lindley thus described the splendid blossom: The flower itself, when it first opens, resembles the white water-lily, of a dazzling white, with its fine leathery petals, forming a goblet of the most elegant proportions; but as the day advances it gradually expands till it becomes nearly flat; towards evening a faint blush becomes visible in the centre, the petals fall back more and more, and at last, about six o'clock, a sudden change occurs; in a few minutes the petals arrange themselves in the form of a snow-white hemisphere, whose edge reposes on the water, and the centre rises majestically at the summit, producing a diadem of rosy points. It then constitutes one of the most elegant objects in nature. Shortly after, the expansion of the central parts proceeding, these points fall back, the stamens unfold in an interior coronet, the stigmas are laid bare, a grateful perfume arises in the air, and the great object of the flower—the fertilization of the seed—is accomplished. Then fold inwards the petals, the flower closes, the fairest of vegetable textures becomes wrinkled, decay begins, and the flower-stalk withdraws itself beneath the water, as if to veil the progress of corruption. But out of this decay arises a new living body; the fruit, curved downward, swells rapidly and in a short time a prickly seed-vessel is observed concealed beneath the floating leaves."

The above descriptions of this wonderful plant will, we think, greatly assist those, who come to admire the Victoria Regia in our parks and are unacquainted with the habits, history and inner life of this vegetable wonder, to get a pretty accurate conception of this interesting object. In addition to all this it may be mentioned that the large, salver-shaped leaves of circular form are capable of supporting the weight of a child from 10 to 12 years of age standing on a board laid across so as to obtain an even balance.

There is no doubt that the head gardeners of both the parks mentioned will make a special effort during the present World's Fair-year to have the Victoria Regia on exhibition in its most perfect and interesting form, so as to be an object of genuine delight to the eye of the multitudes that will throng around the lily-ponds.

The Rockery in Egandale.

FLORICULTURE AT THE WORLD'S COLUMBIAN EXPOSITION.

With the steady march of progress and notably by the aid of the Society of American Florists, and 965 state and local societies and Florists' clubs during the past six years, by the aid of the press, by the aid of exhibitions and by the education which has naturally been obtained from the sources mentioned, the advance of floriculture is one of the wonders of the time.

From a commercial standpoint, the U. S. Census report of commercial floriculture in a digest, is as follows: "In the United States there were 4,659 floral establishments in the census year, 312 of which were owned and conducted by women. The total feet of glass in use in all the establishments was 38,823,247, and the establishments, including fixtures and heating apparatus, were valued at $28,355,722.43. The value of tools and implements used was $1,587,693.93. There were employed 16,847 men and 1,958 women, the combined annual wages amounting to $8,483,657. Fuel cost was $1,160,152.66. Three million, two hundred and forty-five thousand six hundred wholesale, and 17,630.004 retail catalogues are annually issued, while $767,438.21 was paid for postage. $1,161,168.31 for advertising, $354,221.56 for freight, and $554,390.55 for express bills.

The total products were 49,056 253 roses, 38,380,872 hardy plants and shrubs, and 152,835,292 of all other plants, the value of which was $12,036,-477.76, and cut flowers to the amount of $14,175,328.01 were reported as sold. Mr. John Thorpe, chief of the department of floriculture at the World's Fair, has this to say in reference to the floriculture to be exhibited at the Exposition: 'The costliest ideas and the very highest aims are compatible only with the advancement of the profession. Small exhibits can not be expected to be effective. Groups of plants of all kinds will not be shown simply by the hundreds, but in thousands and tens of thousands.

The general massing of the plants will be on such a scale as to astonish even those who are acquainted with what has been accomplished. As a matter of fact, and one that is conceded by those best able to judge, the parks of Chicago have this moment the finest displays of floriculture adornments of all the cities in the world. The brilliant and effective coloring to be seen in the designs at Washington Park and the superior water lily display at Lincoln Park, together with the fine displays at the other parks, have gladdened the hearts and called forth the admiration of hundreds of thousands, remembering what Chicago has, and is now doing for floriculture in her parks.

The floricultural department of the World's Fair must outstrip all previous attempts in all and every one of its branches, even to surpassing the magnificent work here mentioned. This can only be obtained by a determination to eclipse all previous efforts. Not one moment must be given to looking backward. There is no time to look backward. In that magnificent building, Horticultural Hall, will be found space enough to make displays of nearly all exhibits requiring protection. The building is 1,000 feet long with an extreme width of 286 feet. The plan is a central pavilion with two end pavilions each connected to the center pavilion by front and rear curtains, forming two interior courts, each 88 by 270 feet. These courts are beautifully decorated in color and planted with ornamental shrubs and flowers. The center pavilion is roofed by a crystal dome 137 feet in diameter and 113 feet high, under which will be exhibited the tallest palms, bamboos and tree ferns that can be procured. There is a gallery in each of the pavilions. The galleries of the end-pavilions are designed for cafes, the situation and the surroundings being particularly well adapted to recreation and refreshment. The cafes are surrounded by an arcade on three sides, from which charming views of the ground can be obtained. Of various tropical plants there will be large groups of orchids, palms, ferns, and in fact nearly every known decorative species and variety.

Outdoor floriculture will be on such a scale of magnificence as to eclipse all previous efforts, beginning with the showy tulips and hyacinths, ending with chrysanthemums and cosmos. Floriculture must be representative in every sense of the word. However much the cut flowers of roses, carnations, and chrysanthemums are admired and though large numbers of them are produced, they but very imperfectly represent floriculture. Plants of all kinds must be grown and cared for. We should not only have a large variety of plants and flowers for the decoration of dwellings and the adornment of greenhouses, but every plant suitable for the decoration of lawns and gardens. For example, all bulbous plants, all herbaceous plants, and the many beautiful annuals and bienniels, such as are cheaply obtained and easily grown, must have all the encouragement possible at the World's Columbian Exposition. Let us do everything on a scale equal to the magnitude of the undertaking.

I predict that the World's Columbian Exposition will advance floriculture 25 years, and that in ten years from now, I venture to say, that Chicago will come pretty near being the head center of the business."

View In Waldheim Cemetery.

EDWARD S. DREYER.

Mr. Edward S. Dreyer, whose handsome residence is shown on page 103 is one of the most popular and successful business men of Chicago. Besides conducting with Mr. Robert Berger, his amiable partner, the well known banking house of E. S. Dreyer & Co., he was also president of the real estate board of this city, is treasurer of the state private bank association, director and treasurer of Chicago Heights, and was appointed by Mayor Washburne one of the railroad terminal commissioners. He belongs to the public spirited men, who helped to build up the German Old People's Home (Altenheim), the Schiller and Grant monuments in Lincoln Park, the Auditorium, Schiller Theatre, Germania Club building, etc.

Mr. Dreyer is a native of Buckeburg, in Schaumburg-Lippe, Germany, where he was born, August 5, 1844. He was educated in the city of Hameln in Hanover, after which he learned the trade of carriage trimmer. Both of his parents having died when he was yet a child, he went to live with his nearest relatives until he had attained the age of fifteen years. After finishing his schooling he determined to change both his location and his business and accordingly crossed the ocean to America, landing in New York in June, 1864. Upon landing he came directly to Chicago, where he has remained up to the present hour. When he had learned the language of this country and had acquired an insight into the rights and duties of citizenship he entered the employ of Knauer Brothers, real estate dealers, in whose service he remained until January 1, 1870, when, as a reward of merit, he became a member of the firm.

In February, 1873, he withdrew from the partnership and established a real estate business of his own under the name of E. S. Dreyer & Company, which title has been used continuously down to the present time. His office was then located at 72 Dearborn Street, from where it was removed in 1875 to 98 Dearborn Street. The rapid growth of his business soon made it necessary again to remove to more commodious quarters, whereupon he located at 88 Washington Street, where he remained until 1878, when he occupied his present spacious rooms at the northeast corner of Dearborn and Washington Streets. He grew steadily and rapidly in wealth and in popular favor and soon his popularity was not exceeded by that of any other real estate dealer or banker in the city From the time he began, back in 1873, down to the present day, he has invested over $100,000,000, a sum so vast that its magnitude can hardly be comprehended.

So rapidly had Mr. Dreyer amassed money, that in 1877, he founded his mortgage banking business and conducted it in conjunction with his real estate dealings. From 1875 to 1891, Mr. Edward Koch was his business partner, and in 1878 Mr. Robert Berger was also admitted to the partnership and is thus associated at the present time.

Since the great fire in 1871, this firm has built fully two hundred houses in all portions of the city. Mr. Dreyer is a strong democrat and in December 1884 was chosen collector of North Chicago out of thirty-two candidates for the position. In 1888 he was elected school treasurer of Lake View. He is a member of the County Board of Education and a Director of the Public Library.

Mr. Dreyer came to this city poor and friendless; but he was not afraid to work, and where is the German that is? In less than a quarter of a century he has accumulated a large fortune and won an enviable reputation for integrity, honesty and benevolence. His wife was formerly Miss Augusta Billigmann, a native of Keokuk, Iowa, who has presented him with four children; Addie, Lottie, Edward S. Jr. and Florence.

THEO. A. KOCHS.

In illustrating the rapid growth of the City of Chicago and its wonderful development, one of the best examples is the establishment of Theo A. Kochs, manufacturer of Barbers' Supplies, at 158-170 Wells Street. Twenty years ago this business was begun at 217 Fifth Ave. and Mr. Kochs supplied the local barbers with such goods as are needed in this business, but his reputation soon began to spread into adjoining towns and cities and the business rapidly increased. Gradually the whole of the building at 217 Fifth Ave. was occupied and factory space was rented upon the West Side, but the business continued to grow and in 1883 Mr. Kochs found it necessary to erect a building at 158-160 Wells St., into which the entire business, office, store and factory was moved. At the time it seemed that the building would be large enough to meet all requirements, but in 1885 it was necessary to add another story and in 1887 the lot adjoining was built upon, so that the capacity was almost doubled. But even this was not sufficient and in 1890 the building was again enlarged so that now it occupies a frontage of 148 feet on Wells Street and 110 feet on Erie Street, making a total floor space of almost two acres.

In this vast establishment about 250 men are employed in the manufacture of Barbers' Chairs and Furniture, Barbers' Poles, Decorated Shaving Mugs, Cosmetics and Perfumery of all descriptions, and, in fact, *everything* that is required in a modern barber shop. These goods are shipped to all parts of the United States, from Maine to California, to Canada, Mexico, England, Australia and South America, and the establishment that was born twenty years ago now supplies the barbers in every corner of the civilized world.

1873.

1893.

JOHN M. SMYTH BUILDING.

John M. Smyth's new building, to replace that destroyed by fire in April 1891, was begun and completed within a space of about five months. It is one of the finest blocks on the west side, being eight stories in height, having a frontage of 205 feet on Madison street and a depth of 180 feet, and costing $350,000. It is of the so-called, slow-burning mill construction, iron columns and wood being used in the interior and buff Bedford stone and brick for the exterior walls. Two massive arches form the entrance. The store front is provided with the largest plate glass windows in Chicago, each pane being 196 by 120 inches in size. Handsome pillars separate the windows. The main show-room is 120 by 125 feet in area, and the central shipping court, which has a glass, iron-trussed roof, is 55 by 118 feet. Two wings, each 40 by 180 feet, extend back from the main room. Four freight elevators are provided, as well as a number of passenger elevators, run by six engines of 120-horse power. Three thousand, six hundred incandescent electric lights, 250 arc lights and 1,800 gas-jets furnish brillant illumination for every part of the building. Four broad stairways connect the various floors. The entire structure, having a total floor area of 279,000 square feet or six and one-fourth acres, is used for the storing, finishing and uppholstering display and sale of furniture. It is located at 150-166 West Madison street.

Business Notices.

INTERNATIONAL BANK,

110 LA SALLE STREET.

After May 1st, 1893, Security Building,
Cor. Madison and Fifth Ave.

CAPITAL,	-	-	-	$500,000.
SURPLUS,	-	-	-	150,000.

B. LOEWENTHAL, President.

B. NEU, Cashier.

ABENDPOST.

The GREAT
GERMAN DAILY.

229

REGISTER.

233

233

www.ingramcontent.com/pod-product-compliance
Lightning Source LLC
Chambersburg PA
CBHW030313270326
41926CB00010B/1345